Guide to Race Equality

D0715675

WITHDRAWN

Guide to Race Equality in FE

Beulah Ainley

continuum

Continuum International Publishing Group

The Tower Building   80 Maiden Lane, Suite 704
11 York Road   New York
London SE1 7NX   NY 10038

British Library Cataloguing-in-Publication Data
A catalogue record for this book is available from the British Library.

ISBN: 0 8264 8806 4 (paperback)

Typeset by RefineCatch Limited, Bungay, Suffolk
Printed and bound in Great Britain by
Biddles Ltd, King's Lynn, Norfolk

Contents

Acknowledgements

Thanks to all the staff and students who gave me their time for interviews, especially Margaret, Anthony, Errol and Sandra.

Many thanks also to the LSC, the Black Leadership Initiative and UCU for their information and help

Finally to my son, Adam, for his technical assistance and hard work typing this book and to my husband, Patrick, who provided me with lots of information and support.

Dedication to the late Alton Golding

1972–2002

Your wit, intelligence and goodness will always be remembered

Series foreword

THE ESSENITAL FE TOOLKIT SERIES
Jill Jameson
Series Editor

In the autumn of 1974, a young woman newly arrived from Africa landed in Devon to embark on a new life in England. Having travelled half way round the world, she still longed for sunny Zimbabwe. Not sure what career to follow, she took a part-time job teaching EFL to Finnish students. Enjoying this, she studied thereafter for a PGCE at the University of Nottingham in Ted Wragg's Education Department. After teaching in secondary schools, she returned to university in Cambridge, and, having graduated, took a job in ILEA in 1984 in adult education. She loved it: there was something about adult education that woke her up, made her feel fully alive, newly aware of all the lifelong learning journeys being followed by so many students and staff around her. The adult community centre she worked in was a joyful place for diverse multi-ethnic communities. Everyone was cared for, including 90 year olds in wheelchairs, toddlers in the crèche, ESOL refugees, city accountants in business suits and university level graphic design students. In her eyes, the centre was an educational ideal, a remarkable place in which, gradually, everyone was helped to learn to be who they wanted to be. This was the Chequer Centre, Finsbury, ECI, the 'red house', as her daughter saw it, toddling in from the crèche. And so began the story of a long interest in further education that was to last for many years . . . why, if they did such good work for so many, were FE centres so under-funded and unrecognized, so under-appreciated?

It is with delight that, 32 years after the above story began, I write the Foreword to *The Essential FE Toolkit*, Continuum's new book series of 24 books on further education (FE) for teachers and college leaders. The idea behind the *Toolkit* is to provide a comprehensive guide to FE in a series of compact, readable books. The suite of 24 individual books are gathered together to provide the practitioner with an overall FE toolkit in specialist, fact-filled volumes designed to be easily accessible, written by experts with significant knowledge and experience in their individual fields. All of the authors have in-depth understanding of further education. But – '*Why is further education important? Why does it merit a whole series to be written about it?*' you may ask.

At the Association of Colleges' Annual Conference in 2005, in a humorous speech to college principals, John Brennan said that, whereas in 1995 further education was a 'political backwater', by 2005 FE had become 'mainstream', John recalled that, since 1995, there had been '36 separate government or government-sponsored reports or white papers specifically devoted to the post-16 sector'. In our recent regional research report (2006) for the Learning and Skills Development Agency, my co-author Yvonne Hillier and I noted that it was no longer 'raining policy' in FE, as we had described earlier (Hillier and Jameson 2003): there is now a torrent of new initiatives. We thought, in 2003, that an umbrella would suffice to protect you. We'd now recommend buying a boat to navigate these choppy waters, as it looks as if John Brennan's 'mainstream' FE, combined with a tidal wave of government policies will soon lead to a flood of new interest in the sector, rather than end anytime soon.

There are good reasons for all this government attention on further education. In 2004/05, student numbers in LSC council-funded further education increased to 4.2m, total college income was around £6.1 billion, and the average college had an annual turnover of £15m. Further education has rapidly increased in national significance regarding the need for ever greater achievements in UK education and skills training for millions of learners, providing qualifications and workforce training to feed a UK national economy hungrily in competition with other OECD nations. The 120 recommendations of the Foster Review (2005) therefore in the main encourage colleges to focus their work on vocational skills, social inclusion and achieving academic progress. This series is here to consider all three of these areas and more.

The series is written for teaching practitioners, leaders and managers in the 572 FE/LSC-funded institutions in the UK, including FE colleges, adult education and sixth-form institutions, prison education departments, training and workforce development units, local education authorities and community agencies. The series is also written for PGCE/Cert Ed/City & Guilds Initial and continuing professional development (CPD) teacher trainees in universities in the UK, USA, Canada, Australia, New Zealand and beyond. It will also be of interest to staff in the 600 Jobcentre Plus providers in the UK and to many private training organizations. All may find this series of use and interest in learning about FE educational practice in the 24 different areas of these specialist books from experts in the field.

Our use of this somewhat fuzzy term 'practitioners' includes staff in the FE/LSC-funded sector who engage in professional practice in governance, leadership, management, teaching, training, financial and administration services, student support services, ICT and MIS technical support, librarianship, learning resources, marketing, research and development, nursery and crèche services, community and business support, transport and estates management. It is also intended to include staff in a host of other FE services including work-related training, catering, outreach and specialist health, diagnostic additional learning support, pastoral and religious support for students. Updating staff in professional practice is critically important at a time of such continuing radical policy-driven change, and we are pleased to contribute to this nationally and internationally.

We are also privileged to have an exceptional range of authors writing for the series. Many of our series authors are renowned for their work in further education, having worked in the sector for thirty years or more. Some have received OBE or CBE honours, professorships, fellowships and awards for contributions they have made to further education. All have demonstrated a commitment to FE that makes their books come alive with a kind of wise guidance for the reader. Sometimes this is tinged with world-weariness, sometimes with sympathy, humour or excitement. Sometimes the books are just plain clever or a fascinating read, to guide practitioners of the future who will read these works. Together, the books make up a considerable portfolio of assets for you to take with you through your journeys in further education. We hope the experience of reading the books will be interesting, instructive and pleasurable and that experience gained from them will last, renewed, for many seasons.

It has been wonderful to work with all of the authors and with Continuum's UK Education Publisher, Alexandra Webster, on this series. The exhilarating opportunity of developing such a comprehensive toolkit of books probably comes once in a lifetime, if at all. I am privileged to have had this rare opportunity, and I thank the publishers, authors and other contributors to the series for making these books come to life with their fantastic contributions to FE.

Dr Jill Jameson
Series Editor

Series introduction

Race Equality in FE – Beulah Ainley

In January, 2005, when we were taking forward proposals for the Continuum Series of books comprising *The Essential FE Toolkit*, Trevor Phillips, Chair of the Commission for Racial Equality, made an formative keynote speech at the Learning and Skills Development Agency's (LSDA) annual New Year lecture (2005). Mr Phillips called on the further education sector to make more progress in fostering integration for racial equality, saying:

Education is probably the most important site of social and cultural integration we have. Within that, the further education sector has a unique opportunity to bring people together and meet people who are not like them. That is, in my view, the sort of 'added public value' that the further education sector can provide. . . Public value, in this case in education, is about more than just individual value such as exam results, it's about providing a benefit to Britain that is social, cultural and economic. These values should not be overlooked or underestimated.

(CRE, 2005)

The importance of this issue for leaders and managers in the FE system has been highlighted by a number of reports, including those by the Commission for Black Staff in FE, who reported in 2004 that there were only six people out of around 600 principals in the UK who were black, and that just 7% of staff were from ethnic minority groups (Midgley, 2004). In 2005, Ofsted reported that a 'worrying minority' of local education authorities and further education colleges were ' failing to promote race equality' and had 'insufficient procedures in place to tackle racism and harassment among both students and staff'. In two reports on race equality, Ofsted warned that although most colleges were meeting their responsibilities under the Race Relations (Amendment) Act 2000, inspectors had expressed concern about 'a lack of black and ethnic minority staff in senior positions and on governing bodies' (Smithers, 2005).

In this new guidebook on *Race Equality in FE*, Dr Beulah Ainley discusses and promotes the important case for developing and applying best practice in race equality in FE. Beulah is the author of *Black Journalists, White Media* (1998), a book based on the experience of one hundred black journalists working in the British media: she has extensive experience and knowledge of equal opportunities legislation and practice in education and the media.

In *Race Equality in FE*, Beulah reports that racial discrimination remains a serious problem across FE. Although The Race Relations Amendment Act (2000) legally obliges compliance from all public bodies to ensure policies are not racially discriminatory, in practice, colleges have many difficulties implementing this and need guidance and support to do so. Buelah points out that best practice in race equality promotes significant benefits from harmonious inclusive education: she helps us to address, improve and welcome the rewards of racial integration, promoting a series of detailed, helpful actions for college leaders and managers.

The Foster Review of FE (2005), the government White Paper *Further Education: Raising Skills, Improving Life Chances* (2006), and the new Quality Improvement Agency (QIA) are all calling for widespread, rapid improvements in leadership and management across FE. For these to occur, new developments and improvements are needed in promoting diversity and race equality. This timely book on *Race Equality in FE* will help and inspire you make the most of these opportunities in informative, useful ways. I thoroughly commend it to you.

Dr Jill Jameson
Director of Research
School of Education and Training
University of Greenwich
j.jameson@gre.ac.uk

References

CRE (2005) CRE chief calls on further education sector to be agent of integration. Commission for Racial Equality Archived news releases, 18 January 2005. Available online at CRE website, accessed September 24th, 2006: www.cre.gov.uk/Default.aspx.LocID-0hgnew00c. RefLocID-0hg00900c008001002.Lang-EN.htm

Midgley, S. (2004) *Open for all bar some: Why are highly qualified staff from ethnic minorities absent from the top levels of FE colleges.* The Guardian, Simon Midgley, Tuesday April 13, 2004. Available online, accessed September 24th, 2006. http://education.guardian.co.uk/racism/story/0,,1190463,00.html

Smithers, R. (2005) *Colleges 'failing' on race equality.* Guardian Unlimited article: Rebecca Smithers Monday November 21. Available online, accessed September 24th, 2006 at: http://education.guardian.co.uk/further/story/0,,1647527,00.html

Introduction

This book is about race in further education and the implementation of the Race Relations Amendment Act 2000 (RRAA).

Race as an issue, in education, is not new. It began in post-war Britain, when thousands of black immigrants and their children came into the country. The problem of racism, whether institutional or otherwise, in the education system has been the subject of debate for over 40 years.

It has been argued that inequality in society and the education system has resulted in the educational underachievement of black pupils and the underrepresentation of black teachers in education, especially in senior management.

This book looks at race and institutional racism in further education (FE) in conjunction with the requirements of the RRAA. It explains the role of senior management in promoting race equality in colleges, and how best this should be done. It discusses the issues of multicultural education and what is needed to make the curriculum more diverse, for the benefit of all learners.

The text explores the reasons behind the educational underachievement of black learners and the relationship between black students and white teachers. It looks at solutions to racism in FE, giving practical advice on how to promote race equality. This includes monitoring staff and learners, implementing race employment targets, and career development programmes, such as mentoring for black and minority ethnic staff.

The book also recognizes and discusses the importance of race equality training for all staff, including senior managers, governors and other staff. If colleges are to be successful in promoting race equality, they will have to be at least aware of the issues involved. They must also understand why the RRAA is necessary and what their individual responsibility is in helping to eliminate discrimination.

The book reviews research findings, from the 1960s to the present day, on education and race. The publications which report these findings include: *Challenging Racism: Further Education Leading the Way*, the Report of the Commission for Black Staff in Further Education 2002; *Race Equality Work in Further Education Colleges*, March 2003; and *From Issues to Outcomes – Further and Higher Education Institutions, A Guide to Race Equality*, CRE, 2004. Added to this are interviews with students and staff from five further education colleges, who gave their opinions and experiences.

I have many years' experience in FE colleges, first as a student and then later as a lecturer. Consequently, I have first-hand experience, of some of the issues discussed within this book. For example, during my time as a student in further education, I never had a black lecturer, and wondered why there were so few, yet there was an overrepresentation of black cleaners.

Although the book focuses on the responsibilities of senior managers in promoting race equality, it recognizes that everyone who works in FE shares the responsibility to promote race equality. Ultimately the book is for managers, teachers, educational researchers in the fields of race in further and higher education, students and all those interested in equal opportunities.

1 FE and the Race Relations Amendment Act 2000

Despite anti-discrimination legislation from 1962, there is still widespread discrimination in Britain. The Race Relations Amendment Act (RRAA) 2000 is designed to improve the situation in public institutions. It makes clear that educational institutions are responsible for eliminating unlawful racial discrimination and for the promotion of equal opportunities. It is a necessary Act, because the history of race in the British education system is not one to be proud of.

Managers and staff in further education are required not just to understand the Act and put it into practice, but also to understand the issues surrounding race and racism in Britain.

The Act

The RRAA 2000 has general and specific duties. The general duty to promote equal opportunities and take action against racism is strengthened and protects against unlawful discrimination in all public sector bodies, including colleges and universities. It places a duty upon these public institutions to have due regard to the need:

to eliminate unlawful discrimination and to promote equality of opportunity and good relations between persons of different racial groups.

This means that managers of further and higher education institutions cannot, for instance, use the excuse that he or she cannot comply with the duty, because their institution does not have the money.

The specific duties are to help colleges and universities meet the general duty. The Act has placed a number of specific duties upon educational institutions. They are required to:

- prepare and maintain a written race equality policy
- assess the impact of policies on students and staff from different racial groups
- monitor the admission and progression of students and the recruitment and career progression of staff by racial group
- publish the results of monitoring and assessment.

(*The Duty to Promote Race Equality: A Guide for Further and Higher Education Institutions*, CRE 2002: 5)

History of race and education

The debate on race and racism has flourished since the 1960s, when large numbers of black immigrants and their children came to Britain. Immigrant children were seen as 'problems' and were frequently regarded as having a learning disadvantage, because of their language, culture, inadequate parenting and low self-esteem.

British educational policies, between 1958 and the 1980s, have been built around these assumptions. Writers such as Carby (1982), Mullard (1982) and Troyna (1982), have looked at these policies from the point of view of 'assimilation' through to 'cultural pluralism'. Between 1960 and the 1970s the emphasis was on assimilation. The purpose was that immigrant children should embrace English language and culture; this was 'the key to cultural and social assimilation' (Troyna and Williams 1986: 15).

Immigrant children

Racism was never considered to be the reason for black pupils' educational underachievement. Instead, the response was to separate immigrant children from mainstream classes. South Asians and Caribbean children were treated differently. Asian children were placed in separate centres, where they were taught English, without any assessment of whether they could speak English or not. Caribbean pupils were place in mainstream schools, but were removed to educationally subnormal schools, or low-stream classes, if they were judged to be behaving badly (Olser 1997).

Integration policies

This process of segregation restricted black pupils from the mainstream curriculum, examinations and the opportunity to succeed. Yet many local education authorities continued this practice until the late 1980s.

In general, assimilation/integration policies failed, because it was not the immigrants' language and culture that was to be blamed for their educational underachievement, it was racism. This became evident as a result of the 1958 anti-black riots in Nottingham and Notting Hill.

Policy changes

From the late 1970s, some policy-makers on race and education began to recognize and accept that there was white hostility towards black immigrants and began to focus on social and cultural diversity. For some local education authorities, this amounted to no more than the tokenistic introduction of steel bands and curry. This was obviously an inadequate way of dealing with structural racism.

The Rampton/Swann Committee set up in 1979 believed that multicultural education was intended to address the educational needs and achievements of black and minority ethnic (BME) pupils.

In *Education for All* (1985), the Swann report explained what the committee meant by 'good education'. The authors included in this definition:

- the use of teaching materials which are multicultural in content and global in perspective
- the provision of opportunities for pupils to identify and challenge racism
- the inclusions of effective political education, with scope to consider how power is exercised and by whom
- the identification and removal of practices and procedures which directly and indirectly work against pupils from ethnic groups.

The report stressed that these recommendations should also be taken up by schools in all white areas, acknowledging the potential benefits of multicultural education for white children. The RRAA 2000 is the latest set of recommendations to the education system in an effort to eliminate racial discrimination.

Who is responsible for promoting the Act in FE?

The law says that college governing bodies:

are legally responsible for making sure the institution complies with the Act and meets its duties, including the general duty and the specific duties.

(CRE 2002: 29)

Despite this, it is managers who should be committed to race equality and provide effective leadership and direction by:

seeking to eliminate discrimination and create a working and learning environment, based on positive relations between members of different racial groups.

Who should be consulted?

The manager or managers responsible for the college's race policy should draw up a list of people to be consulted. It should include representatives from staff and student unions, the CRE, the college principal, heads of departments and non-teaching staff. Everyone in the college should be involved and should know what the RRAA 2000 is and what their collective and individual responsibilities are.

What is a race policy?

It is a description of how the college is going to prevent racial discrimination and promote equality of opportunities.

The policy should 'reflect the character and circumstances of the institution' and deal, with the areas that promote 'equality of opportunity and good Race Relations' (*A Guide for Further and Higher Education Institutions*, CRE 2002: 13).

Areas to be covered by the race equality policy should include:

- The college's values, such as mutual respect between students and staff, staff and staff, and students and other students.

- A clear and consistent approach to bad behaviour, such as racial and sexual harassment and theft.
- A commitment to a multicultural curriculum, because without it the college will not be able to promote equal education of all its students.
- An explanation of the training that teachers will receive to help them teach a more inclusive curriculum.
- A clear outline of the responsibilities of managers for taking the lead in promoting the race equality policy in all areas of the college.
- A commitment by the race manager to delegate work to other managers and heads of departments
- The college's commitment to promoting and providing positive messages and images of BME groups inside and outside of the college.
- A promise to consult with BME staff and student representatives when developing the race equality policy and action plan.
- A clear outline of the responsibilities of governors for ensuring that the college reflects the diversity of the community that it serves.
- A strategic plan that includes a commitment to race equality.

Staff
- An equality training programme for managers, governors and all staff, teaching and non-teaching; should be part of the college's strategic plan.
- The college's commitment to the monitoring, recruitment, retention and promotion of BME staff.
- A commitment to set targets, based upon the analysis of monitoring information − a procedure vital in addressing the underrepresentation of BME staff in further education, especially in managerial positions.

Students
- Monitoring of recruitment, retention and achievement of learners.
- Targets based upon the results of the monitoring information.

This action will help to address BME student underachievement and widen course choices.

- A commitment that all students will receive a written copy of the college's race equality policy, which should also be displayed in student union offices, notice-boards, learning resource and support centres.
- An outline of actions that can be taken by students and staff who experience discrimination.
- A promise to ensure that all providers of work placements will receive a summary of the college's race policy under the RRAA 2000 and that they have agreed to the conditions of the policy.
- Arrangements to monitor teaching and learning, including language and cultural needs.
- Plans to build race equality into the college's policy of planning and development.
- Arrangements for putting the race policy into practice, including a timetable for regular reviews of its aims and actions taken.
- Plans for monitoring and assessing progress towards meeting any race equality targets set and the race equality duty under the RRAA 2000.

The college will have to include in its commitments to racial equality an annual publication of a summary of results of its monitoring of race information and what action has been taken, or what will be done based upon these results.

Communicating the race policy

Communication and consultation are necessary if FE is to successfully promote race equality and diversity. It is the provision and exchange of information that allows stakeholders and colleges to be properly informed about their respective issues and developments. There are two specific areas of communication that need to be looked at:

- What is the information provided?
- How and who is it going to be communicated to?

(*Race Equality Toolkit*, UCEA 2004)

A business case for equality and diversity communication

By communicating and consulting with stakeholders, e.g. staff, learners, governors, trade union and BME groups, FE colleges will be seen to be promoting and recognizing equality and diversity:

- it will improve staff morale and trust
- increase BME staff retention
- improve the talent base of the college
- create a positive working and learning environment.

This leads to:

- increased economic productivity, as more BME staff and learners will be wanting to come to the college.
- better value for money
- a positive image of the college from outside agencies and other educational institutions
- reducing the risk of legal action against the college from the CRE and individuals.

Methods of communication

A variety of communication methods need to be used. They may be spoken, written or through photographs. Methods which might be used include:

- group meetings
- conferences
- inter-departmental meetings
- research and surveys
- meetings with local and focus groups
- formal and informal verbal communication
- written materials including notes, journals, newsletters, notices or emails
- meetings with faith groups inside and outside the college
- networking with other colleges and sharing good practice with them.

(UCEA 2004)

A model race policy for FE

Our commitment

- The college celebrates and values the diversity brought to its work-force by individuals, and believes that the college will benefit from engaging staff from a variety of racial, ethnic and national back-grounds, thus allowing it to meet the needs of a diverse student population within a multicultural society. The college will treat all employees and students with respect and dignity, and seek to pro-vide a working environment free from racial discrimination, harass-ment or victimization.
- The college will create a positive working and learning environment where there are positive relations between members of different racial groups. To this end, the college undertakes to provide training and support for staff, to consult with black staff about their experi-ence of the working environment, and to provide diverse images in any material which it produces for staff.

Meeting our duties

We will seek to ensure that:

- Governors, staff, learners and their sponsors (including work-placement providers) are aware of our racial equality policy and the action needed for its implementation.
- Staff, learners and their sponsors (including work-placement providers) are aware of the value placed upon equal opportunity and that action will be taken in the event of any breach of the policy.
- Governors and staff have access to comprehensive information, which assists them to plan, implement and monitor actions to carry out their responsibilities under the policy.

We will also ensure the college's publicity materials present appropriate and positive messages about minority racial groups.

Monitoring progress

- The monitoring process will be used to ensure that staff are treated equally in terms of promotion, staff development, grading, etc.
- To inform the setting of targets and the measurement of our pro-gress in achieving them, we will collect and analyse the following information by racial group origin:

Learners
- racial group profiles of learners
- applications, and success and failure rates for admission to programmes
- retention rates
- achievement rates and the curriculum
- work placements including success rates, satisfaction levels and job offers
- disciplinary action
- complaints by learners or their sponsors
- student surveys.

Employees
- racial group profiles of employees by grade/salary scales and type of work
- job application rates
- selection success rates
- type of contract (permanent, temporary)
- training/staff development
- promotion application and success rates
- disciplinary/capability proceedings
- grievances
- exit surveys.

The college undertakes, once the results of monitoring are available, to consider targets to reduce any disadvantage suffered by ethic minority employees and learners. If monitoring reveals that specific racial minority groups are especially disadvantaged, some targets may relate to those specific groups. The targets will be published annually in an Action Plan.

Publicizing our policy and progress
To the public (including learners, work-placement providers and staff)

- Our commitment to racial equality will be highlighted in our prospectus, annual report and annual financial statement.
- A summary of the results of our monitoring information will be included in our annual report and annual financial statements, where this does not breach individual confidentiality.
- Staff and all learners will receive a summary of this policy. Copies of

the policy will be on display in the learning resources and student support centres and form part of the staff handbook.

Work placement
All work placement providers will receive a summary of their responsibilities under the policy and will signify their understanding and agreement to these responsibilities.

Review and consultation
This policy will be reviewed on a regular basis, in accordance with legislative developments and the need for good practice, by the College Equality Forum. As part of the review the Forum will seek and take into account the views of stakeholders, including learners and work-placement providers, using the local consultation/negotiating arrangements within the College, and appropriate equality bodies (i.e. CRE).

Implementation
The college, working in partnership with the recognized trade unions and employee representatives, will seek to ensure that all staffing policies and procedures (e.g. Recruitment and Selection Procedure) are non-discriminatory, and that the monitoring and positive action processes are regularly reviewed and monitored.

Discrimination on the grounds of religion and belief

As to religion, I hold it to be the indispensable duty of government to protect all conscientious professors thereof, and I know of no other business which government hath to do therewith.
(Tom Paine, *Common Sense*, 1737–1809)

White British people are becoming increasingly secular. Although Christians, very few attend church regularly, except for special occasions such as weddings, christenings and funerals. However, while religion is becoming less important to white British people, for some BME groups religion is a significant factor of their lives.

Why we need policy in FE against discrimination on religion or beliefs

- It is difficult for those with secular views to understand the need for laws against religious discrimination.
- Racism and religion overlap, but they are not the same.
- There is a problem when trying to deal with religious discrimination under the RRAA 2000: many groups and individuals from BME communities identify mainly with their religion, rather than their racial origin. Muslims have argued that policies based on ethnic frames are not adequate to their self-understanding (UCU 2002: 5).
- There is a European Employment Directive which requires all member states to introduce domestic legislation outlawing discrimination on the grounds of religion or belief.
- Article 9 of the Human Rights Act helps to protects freedom of religion and belief. It states that:

  Everyone has the right to freedom of thought, conscience and religion; this right includes freedom to change his belief or religion and freedom, either alone or in community with others and, in public or private, to manifest his religion or belief, in worship, teaching, practice and observance.

- Some members of minority faith have specific needs in the workplace so that they can practise their religion. Some colleges and HE institutions largely ignore these needs. British society has been based historically around Christianity. There is no special time for prayers built into the day at work because Christians do not need it.

Model policy on culture, religion and belief

1. Statement of intent

The college celebrates and values the diversity brought to its workforce through individuals, and aims to create an environment where the cultural, religious and non-religious beliefs of all its employees are respected.

Through the implementation of the relevant policies and procedures the college seeks to ensure that

a) recruitment and selection are based entirely on relevant criteria, which do not include religious belief or non-belief

b) members of any religion or none are treated with equal dignity and fairness
c) underrepresented groups in society are encouraged to apply for jobs
d) where possible, appropriate services are provided to meet the cultural and religious needs of all employees

The right to freedom of thought, conscience and religion is absolute, but the right to manifest beliefs is qualified by the need to protect the rights and freedoms of others.

2. Dress code

- The college imposes no dress code on its employees, and welcomes the variety of appearance brought by individual styles and choices.
- The only limitations to the above are:
    a) health and safety requirements may mean that for certain tasks specific items of clothing such as overalls, protective clothing, etc. need to be worn. If such clothing produces a conflict with an individual's religious belief, the issue will be sympathetically considered by the line manager, with the aim of finding a satisfactory compromise
    b) dress should conform to the current majority view in our society of what constitutes decency
    c) wearing of clothing displaying slogans which are discriminatory (e.g. racist or sexist slogans) is forbidden.

3. Cultural and religious observance

i) The college will ensure that all staff know that if they have special prayer requirements, they should put in a request to line managers who will ensure that a suitable place for prayer, plus ablution facilities if required, will be made available.
ii) All staff, regardless of religious belief or non-belief, are required to work for the contracted hours agreed per week. There is considerable flexibility over when these hours are worked.

4. Leave for religious festivals

Those practising other religions or none have an absolute right to book three days of their holiday entitlement on the dates of most significance to them. Any further requests for holiday entitlement to be taken at times of religious significance will be treated sympathetically.

The number of annual leave days overall will remain the same as in the contract of employment, for all staff, of any religious belief or none.

Implementation and responsibilities

- All line managers are responsible for familiarizing themselves with this policy, and for following it in matters such as requests for leave.
- All individual staff are responsible for familiarizing themselves with this policy, for informing appropriate staff of their particular requirements, and for making up any time lost as a result of cultural/religious observance.
- Any member of staff who feels their line manager is not treating them fairly in accordance with this policy should first try to resolve the matter by discussion and, if that fails, take the matter up with their head of department. If that fails, the grievance procedure can be used.

Summary

In this chapter we looked at the RRAA 2000: what the Act states and the responsibilities of senior managers in FE to promote it. This led to examining why the Act was needed and the history of race and education. We found that BME children have experienced institutional racism in the British educational system since the 1950s.

We then explained the importance of a race policy for FE in promoting race equality. This is a requirement called for by the RRAA 2000 for colleges and other educational institutions.

We gave practical guidance on what the policy should contain and who should be consulted in drawing up the policy. We also looked at discrimination against religion and beliefs, pointing out that although the policy on race overlaps that of religion and belief they are not the same. A separate policy against discrimination on the basis of religion and belief has been added.

2 Race awareness in FE

It does not matter how good a race policy is and who has helped to draw it up; if FE managers, governors and staff are not committed to putting policy into practice, nothing will change.

Agenda for change

The Race Relations Amendment Act 2000 is one of the strongest anti-discriminatory Acts in Britain. It is based upon the fact that the only way to achieve race equality is by providing practical ways of tackling racism. The Commission for Black Staff in Further Education recommended an agenda for change, which states that in order to achieve real and lasting changes, colleges are urged to:

- raise awareness of the Commission's findings and recommendations
- make sure that action is taken, where necessary, to eliminate discriminatory practices and procedures
- take proactive steps to change attitudes and organizational cultures
- provide training to ensure that staff are sensitized to identify and deal with institutional racism
- acknowledge, promote and share good practice in the sector
- set ambitious, but realistic targets and time frames for change.

(*Summary Report of the Commission for Black Staff in Further Education*, 2002, chapter 5)

Broken promises

In 2002 colleges made a commitment and agreed that:

- senior management would be accountable for implementing race equality policies

- staff development would be available to ensure compliance with the legislation
- action would be taken in cases of race discrimination
- they would set equality targets and carry out ethnic monitoring of students and staff and publish regular reports with the results of monitoring

(*Implementing the Race Relations Amendment Act*, UCU/Unison Guide, 2004)

Despite the commitment made by colleges to implement the RRAA, most are not doing enough to bring about significant changes to race equality.

So bad is the situation that in 2005 Trevor Phillips, Chairman of the Commission for Racial Equality, warned colleges to 'Reform or else' and he went on to say that he will place compliance orders on colleges who are not promoting race equality (Clancy 2005).

What is 'race'?

To understand the root of the problem we have to first look at what 'race' is. Race is a social categorization, based upon different physical characteristics, but there are no important biological differences between ethnic groups. Race becomes an issue when some groups are treated differently, because of these different physical characteristics and beliefs about genetic inferiority. Racism is also the action taken by an individual, or a group, whether deliberate or unintentional, against another person, resulting in racial discrimination. There are many types of racism: individual, institutional, cultural and religious.

Racism

The anti-racist slogan advocates that prejudice and power equal racism. It is believed that racism can only occur, 'when a racially prejudiced individual or group has the power to act out that prejudice in a harmful discriminatory way' (Leicester 1993: 17). Therefore the dominant group has the power to discriminate systematically against members of a less powerful group.

Although, in this instance, we are talking about racism based on colour, racism is not always about this, but can be religious and cultural. However, prejudice and discrimination, based on colour, is the building ground for racism at other levels, in religious and cultural terms, for example, the increase in Islamophobia since 9/11.

Prejudice

Prejudice, then, is the first ingredient of racism. It is when an individual or group has some preconceived opinion or bias against someone or something. The information about that person or thing may possibly have been formed by what they have seen, read or heard, or been told by family and friends. Despite the fact that this information may be incorrect, inadequate or biased, it may be believed to be true. Sometimes these may be the only sources available about a person or groups and, as such, a distorted view is presented.

The result of this preconceived idea is that a stereotypical picture may emerge of a particular group and they may then be judged by this 'established set of expectations' (Leicester 1993: 17). Racial prejudices are formed in this way from ignorance and the existence of stereotypes of different groups of people. The media and educational institutions often reinforce these stereotypes.

Institutional racism

Institutional racism is different from the anti-racism slogan that 'prejudice and power equals racism', in that the individuals involved in institutional racism are acting as functionaries of an institution which need not involve prejudicial intention at all.

The Macpherson Inquiry (1999) found that the term had been subject to 'much debate' and found it dangerous to allow the term to be used in order to express overall criticism of the police, or any other organization, without addressing its meaning. The inquiry came to the conclusion that 'institutional racism' was:

The collective failure of an organisation to provide an appropriate and professional service to people because of their colour, culture or ethnic origin.

(*Macpherson Report* 1999: 7)

Colour blindness

Many organizations, public or otherwise, fail to recognize that their actions or behaviour can result in racial discrimination. They believe that everyone is treated the same. Even when the problem is brought to their attention and laws like the RRAA 2000 are established, they resist change either partially or completely.

Media

The media are similar to colleges and other educational institutions, where they refuse to believe that there is a problem. A research study in 1994 on the British media did not find a single editor who agreed that the industry was guilty of institutional racism, although evidence proved otherwise.

In large urban cities such as London, Birmingham, Manchester and Leeds, where high numbers of black people have lived for more than 50 years, most newspapers had either no BME journalists, or only a token few. When asked why, editors claimed that black people did not apply for jobs. This is an exhausted excuse for not doing anything to change the situation. When these editors were asked if they had monitored applications, none had, so they in fact had no idea how many applicants were black (Ainley 1994).

How racism works in FE/HE

Whether racism is intentional or not, it's the outcomes rather than the intentions that are important. If the result of unintentional racism is harmful to a particular group or individual, then it is discriminatory.

Although the McPherson inquiry looked at police action, it pointed out that institutional racism was more widespread and was found in other public services such as 'education and housing'.

Like other institutions, further and higher education organizations are guilty of institutional racism. For example, many FE/HE institutions are not promoting their race policy if they have one. They have Eurocentric male-dominated curricula which ignore the contribution of BME groups and women. Many FE colleges and HE institutions still have recruitment policies and procedures which discriminate against BME groups.

Racial bullying and harassment

Harassment and bullying is a serious offence, whether it is racially motivated or not. The Commission for Black Staff in Further Education found that black staff 'are very used to racial comments from white colleagues'.

A black staff member who gave evidence to the Commission explained:

After only a few weeks at the college, I began to experience racist innuendo and horseplay. Over four years there were some 40 incidents, including people urinating in my coffee and threats of physical violence.

(*The Full Report of the Commission for Black Staff in Further Education* 2003a, chapter 3: 55)

Employer responsibilities
The college has a general duty, also covered in Health and Safety legislation, to provide a safe and healthy working environment, which includes protection against bullying and harassment. Harassment on the grounds of a person's sex, race or disability, can be considered discrimination under the Sex Discrimination Act 1975, Race Relations Act 1976 and Disability Discrimination Act 1995 respectively.

It is unlawful to discriminate against someone in the workplace on the grounds of his or her religion or belief, or his or her sexual orientation under the following legislation: Employment Equality (Religion or Belief) Regulations 2003 and Employment Equality (Sexual Orientation) Regulations 2003.

Definitions and examples of bullying and harassment
Bullying can be defined as offensive, intimidating, malicious, insulting, or humiliating behavioural abuse of power or authority which

attempts to undermine an individual or group of employees and which may cause them to suffer stress.

Bullying and harassment may include:

- spreading malicious rumours, insulting or taunting someone (particularly on the grounds of race, sex, sexual orientation and religion or belief)
- verbal intimidation, e.g. threats, shouting and swearing at someone, racist or sexist taunts
- overbearing supervision or other misuse of power or position
- ridiculing or demeaning someone
- making someone the butt of jokes to humiliate them in front of others
- preventing individuals from progressing by intentionally blocking promotion or training opportunities because of their race or religion

(Harassment at Work: How to deal with it,
UCU 1995)

An example of one college's anti-bullying and harassment policy

Introduction

The college supports the right of all employees to be treated with dignity and respect at work and is committed to providing a safe and supportive working environment free from all forms of bullying and harassment. The college further recognizes its responsibility to protect the victims of any bullying and harassment and to deal effectively with such behaviour.

Employees will be made aware of this policy and will be expected to comply. Bullying and harassment will not be tolerated and such behaviour will be dealt with as appropriate under the college's disciplinary procedures.

- Bullying and harassment may be treated as a disciplinary offence and action taken as appropriate.
- Managers should be aware of the college policy on bullying and harassment and ensure it is applied effectively.
- The college will treat seriously any complaint of bullying or harassment that is made and will offer counselling support

through Care First for the complainant and alleged bully/harasser when appropriate.

- All complaints will be investigated in a confidential manner. When a complaint is upheld steps will be taken by the college to prevent any further instances occurring.
- The college will protect an employee at work who makes a complaint of bullying or harassment.

Employee responsibilities

- Employees should treat all with whom they work with dignity and respect in accordance with the staff code of conduct.
- Employees should not bully or harass other employees, students or members of the public.
- Employees should be encouraged to take action in accordance with the policy if bullying or harassment occurs.
- Employees can be held personally liable for acts of harassment and may have to pay compensation. This is separate to, and in addition to, any compensation that the college would have to pay.

Training

Staff will be briefed on the bullying and harassment policy as part of the induction process. Training/awareness will be provided to managers to ensure they have the necessary knowledge and skills to communicate and operate the policy effectively ensuring compliance with the legislation.

Monitoring and review

The college will maintain anonymous records of all reported cases of bullying and harassment dealt with through the bullying and harassment procedure and how they are resolved. The records will include the following:

- the number of formal complaints made
- the outcomes of the complaints
- the time taken to complete the process.

This monitoring information will be used by the equal opportunities committee to evaluate the effectiveness of the college's policy and procedures in handling cases of bullying and harassment.

Race equality training in FE

Training for equality has been fraught with problems since it came into being in the 1980s. Training initiatives include racism awareness training (RAT) and anti-racism training. Racism awareness training has been criticized and marginalized over the years and the reason has seemed to be because:

such training is focused on white people which at least represents ... a shift of emphasis and it aims to produce an active awareness of Racism in its persona and institutional forms.

(Chris Gaine 1998: 104)

Yet in order for colleges to meet the legal requirement of the RRAA 2000, race equality training is essential, not on an ad hoc basis, but in a well organized manner, taking care of the contents and delivery. Training and refresher courses should be given to staff at least once a term.

Race equality training is necessary, not just for the explanation of the college's statutory duties, but to inform and educate staff on why the RRAA 2000 is necessary. This means discussing the issue of 'structural racism'.

What is race awareness training?

Race awareness training, which was introduced in the 1980s, has the overall objective to help whites become aware of how Racism affects their lives and to help them change their lives and to help them change their racist attitudes and behaviour (Katz 1978).

Race awareness training in the 1980s tended to focus too much on individual attitudes and less on institutional racism. This early race awareness training was criticized for defining racism as a 'white problem' and because some argued that this approach often 'incurred feelings of guilt, defensiveness or resentment amongst white people and scepticism from Black people' (*The Commission for Black Staff* 2002).

What race equality training should cover
- It should challenge racial discrimination on both the individual and structural levels, as you cannot have one without the other.

- Training should focus on what individuals and organizations can do to bring about change in practices and procedures.
- Structural racism should be discussed, e.g. BME groups and their historical relationships with Britain and immigration after the Second World War. This background information is important, as it gives an understanding of why the RRAA 2000 is necessary.
- The legal obligations of the college to promote race equality and the individual responsibility of learners, staff, governors and stakeholders.
- The benefits to the college and individuals of implementing race equality policies.
- The challenging of racial stereotypes and the provision of good practices.

Equality training for managers

Most white managers, before training, have very little knowledge about race and equality; if they do, it is usually only in theory. Managers are not to be blamed for this situation, since their education, training and experience may not have opened them to the information and challenges of discrimination.

It is therefore vital that managers and senior staff in further education have equality training, as they are the ones who are primarily responsible for promoting race equality.

Training session for managers

- Managers should be given comprehensive information about the RRAA 2000 and their legal responsibilities in promoting it. Several training sessions may be needed.
- An expert in legal and race issues should lead the sessions.
- It should be stressed that for a successful race programme managers need to know more than just how to draw up a policy: they need to know how to put policies into practice.
- Training should explain a convincing business case for race equality. This includes items such as avoiding expensive legal action, e.g. if colleges are accused of racial discrimination, harassment and bullying, or have compliance orders issued against them by the CRE.
- Training should raise managers' awareness of structural and

institutional racism, its effects and what managers need to do to raise the awareness of staff and learners in challenging discrimination in the college.

- Managers should be trained to recognize race equality as part of the college's core values and an integral part of the strategic and operational planning.
- Training should include the following anti-discrimination legislation
  - The Special Educational Needs and Disability Act (SENDA), 2001, which amends the Disability Discrimination Act (DDA), 1995.
  - The Sex Discrimination Act, 1975
  - The Human Rights Act, 1998
  - The European Directive which requires member states to outlaw discrimination in employment on the grounds of sexual orientation, religion, belief or age by 2006.

Cultural diversity training

Cultural diversity training should focus on the cultural and religious differences we have in colleges and other educational institutions. Diversity consists of both visible and non-visible differences and covers factors such as gender, age, race, food, clothes, disability and work.

Colleges have to harness these differences and use them positively. The effect will be to eliminate discrimination, creating an equal and safe environment for all students and staff.

Cultural and diversity training should:

- Provide information about the cultural and religious differences of students and staff, in colleges and society in general.
- Explain religious obligations and festivals, e.g. Eid, Diwali, black history month.
- Challenge stereotypes and assumptions about BME cultures and religions.
- Include speakers who represent the students, staff, local community groups and voluntary organizations. They can speak from personal experience and relate to the problems BME groups face in FE and society.
- Encourage the celebration of diversity by giving BME

learners and staff time off for festivals and celebrations. Other staff and learners should be encouraged to take part in any celebrations which are appropriate.

- Encourage colleges to advertise religious festivals and other celebrations on notice boards and in student and staff news-letters. This will be seen as a public statement of the college's commitment to race equality.
- Put forward the business case for cultural diversity training. It will bring better understanding between the different races and help to break down barriers.
- Raise awareness of managers and staff to the needs of BME staff and learners.
- Encourage colleges to recruit a more diverse staff who will be able to meet the needs of all students.
- Be held in colleges in white areas. This is important, because most staff and students from these areas have little or no knowledge about cultural diversity.

Race equality training for teaching and non-teaching staff

Preparation

For training to be successful, preparations should be made weeks before the day of training. The training programme should be planned thoroughly to ensure that participants are properly briefed and know what is required of them. All participants need to know the date, time and venue for the training in good time.

Dietary needs should be catered for. If the event is to be held at the college, the name and number of the room should be stated. Managers, governors and speakers are all busy people: if you want good attendance, it would be best to inform people as early as possible.

The trainer

The facilitator should be someone with training, experience and ability, specifically in race and equality issues. He or she will be responsible for guiding the day's training in the direction it is meant to be taking. Preparation should involve supplying partici-pants with background information, such as papers, books, informa-tion on the RRAA 2000 and other reading. All should be sent to participants in advance in order for them to read, digest and hopefully get a better understanding of the issues before the day of training.

Speakers
Although the facilitator should be an experienced trainer, he or she will need help from external speakers, for example representatives from the CRE, staff unions, the LSC and the college equality and diversity group if there is one. The point of having these speakers is that they bring expertise and knowledge about their subject. For example, the CRE representative will be able to explain the legal requirements of the RRAA 2000 and what managers and governors need to do to implement the Act.

Background information
Outside speakers should be supplied with background information about the college before the training day so that they will have a better understanding of the college's needs. For example, the college may already have a race policy and an equal opportunities group, but they may not be carrying out any monitoring. The trainer may therefore need to know how to monitor and assess the monitoring carried out. It might be that the college wants guidance on all aspects of the RRAA 2000, because none of the managers have any equality experience. Whatever the case, training should be geared towards the specific needs of the college involved.

External trainers
It might be better to use external trainers/facilitators, unless the college has someone with specialist skills in equalities training and knowledge of race equality issues in education. They will also need knowledge of the legal statutory framework and the implications of this for FE. It is unlikely that most colleges will have someone with the expertise and the confidence to run a training course. A lot of stress and discomfort can be experienced by staff when training close colleagues and teammates on a potentially controversial subject. In-house trainers will need someone to help with their existing workload alongside the research and planning needed to carry out race equality training.

Finding the trainer

However, getting the right external trainer is not always going to be easy. They have to be given careful briefs as to what is expected of them and these should be agreed in writing, as well as verbally. You have to be sure that the trainer has the necessary experience and can deliver training in the right style and that he or she will be able to follow your brief. Trainers should understand that their participants are formally educated people, who are knowledgeable about education and politics but may not know a great deal about race issues.

Information

An external trainer should be given the following:

- Background information about the college, before he or she is hired. This should include the college's values and race equality statement, if they have one.
- Staff and learners' profiles, including ethnic origin, along with the results of any monitoring and assessment reviews and details of the curriculum on offer.
- Feedback from recent inspections of the college and the results of staff and student surveys highlighting key issues of concern.

It is best to get an outside trainer who has been recommended by more than one person, but better still one whom the contract manger has seen in action.

Contract

Trainers should be issued with a standard contract in writing and given a duplicate copy. The contract should outline details of training, such as delivery dates, times, target groups, minimum and maximum group sizes. They should also be told the anticipated training outcomes, the requirements needed to comply with the college's race and equality and health and safety policies and information regarding the evacuation of training rooms, in the event of an emergency. The contract should also contain details about the college's expectations regarding the trainer's confidentiality, language, behaviour, presentation, delivery of materials and other professional standards. Within the contract there should also be confirmation of the venue and any accommodation and equipment required.

Trainer's duty
The trainer should supply the college with relevant information too. This should include information about employment experience and at least two references from clients concerning the trainer's training ability and experience, especially in FE. Trainers should also provide a copy of the training programme that has been agreed, copies of handouts and resources to be distributed or collected in advance, along with the details of travel arrangements, contact details, including email addresses and mobile phone numbers and bank details for payment purposes.

Equipment
Films and videos can be used as part of the training session. They are useful in explaining concepts and for generating debates. The college might also want to produce a video of the proceedings, which could then be used for future training purposes. Information about the trainer could also be posted on the college's website. It is important that the course participants and outside speakers also include BME groups.

Training day
The following guidelines may help with the organization of a race equality training day in an FE college:

- a welcome address with information about the day's programme should be included
- external speakers and trainers should be formally introduced and subjects introduced generally
- after the formal introduction, participants should be given time to go to workshops for which they had previously registered
- each workshop should deal with a particular aspect of race equality
- workshops should have between five and ten people
- training should be linked to examples of good practice and the use of check lists
- there should be clear aims and objectives
- there should be structured discussions on the RRAA 2000 and the college's legal duty to promote it

- ground rules should be set which promote mutual respect and support trainers and participants
- time should be allowed for question-and-answer sessions and all participants should be encouraged to join in the discussions
- sufficient time should be left for evaluation and feedback to be given
- there should be adequate breaks given for refreshments, lunch and tea, etc.
- smoking should not be permitted during the meeting and all mobile phones should be turned off.

Case study 1

A college, after several complaints, realized that it needed to take into consideration the needs of various religions and spiritual groups which were represented in the student and staff community. It was apparent that the college had a Christian focus and ethos and was not inclusive of other faiths and their followers, who also needed space for spiritual support.

The college sought help from different faiths and the local community. It held discussions and listened to the comments and recommendations of various groups. As a result, the college received a lot of information about the different faiths represented and how they could get leaders involved. This led to the college providing multi-faith facilities, where the leaders and representatives of any faith could be available to the student and staff population.

This change was communicated to all students and staff via notice boards, the student union, the college website, the annual report, community and equality focus groups.

Case study 2

A college monitored its canteen to see who used it, but had no information from the people who did not use it, or from any equality group within the college. The college decided to send out a questionnaire to those who did not use or rarely used the canteen to find out the different experiences of students and staff.

The results showed that staff and students who had diabetes or were vegetarian, Muslim or Jewish were not adequately catered for. There were hardly ever any fresh fruit and vegetables and the canteen never used halal or kosher products. These were the reasons given for why some did not use the canteen.

The college acted upon the information gathered. They set up a focus group which communicated with various faith and religious groups to gain an understanding of the needs of some BME groups. They also received information from a dietician about healthy eating and nutrition. As a result, the college redesigned its menu to include kosher and halal foods, more fresh fruit, vegetables, and low fat and salt options.

Case study 3

A college needed more BME staff to get involved in its race equality policy and practices. It publicized its request on the college's notice board, newsletters, websites and in local trade union offices.

The publicity emphasized the importance of all staff involvement in the process of promoting race equality. It particularly wanted the active involvement of BME staff who are underrepresented in all sectors of the college, especially management.

The college recognized the importance of BME staff in the process of monitoring the impact of the race equality policy. The response to the communications was exceptional: within days most BME staff had made contact; this included part-time and hourly paid workers. They suggested a meeting with the senior manager in charge of co-coordinating race equality, the principal and heads of department.

The meeting was well attended and views shared were both honest and open. BME staff explained how they had been marginalized and stereotyped in the college for years and not given the same opportunities as white colleagues. They welcomed the college race equality policy and were willing to work with the college to bring about change.

As a result a black staff focus group was set up, which communicated its views and ideas to the race equality managers, helping the college to promote race equality policies.

Summary

This chapter discussed race and racism and how institutional racism is used in FE and HE institutions to discriminate against BME staff and students.

We argued that if race equality is to be successful in FE, then all staff and students need to have race awareness training. We gave practical advice on what training should cover and how it should be carried out.

3 Black students: underachievement

Underachievement

Data from DfES 2002 has shown that black and minority ethnic (BME) learners are underachieving in comparison to their white colleagues. They get lower grades, despite marked improvements in their achievement.

Black pupils, especially those of Caribbean descent, have become synonymous with educational underachievement. While there are many causes for underachievement, research evidence indicates that the main one is likely to be institutional racism within the British education system, played out in policies and practices.

Racism and underachievement

Several research studies on this, including Mac an Ghaill 1988, Gilborn 1990, Sewell 1997 and The Education Commission 2005, have all concluded that racism is to be blamed for the educational underachievement of black students. But what they also observed was the problematic relationship between white teachers and black learners.

The involvement of teachers in the educational underachievement of black students was first observed in 1971, when Bernard Coard, then teaching in London, published his book, *How the West Indian Child is Made Educationally Subnormal in the British Education System*. Coard's book responded to the concerns of the West Indian community at the number of their children being placed in educationally subnormal (ESN) schools. Coard described the process of the self-fulfilling prophecy and for the first time teachers were implicated in the underachievement of black pupils.

White teachers, black students

Coard argued in his book that white teachers, as part of a racist society, had low expectations of black pupils and so underestimated their abilities. He explained:

Most teachers absorb the brainwashing that everybody else in society has absorbed that Black people are inferior and less intelligent than white people. Therefore the Black child is expected to do less well in school.

(Coard 1971: 25)

Racial stereotypes

Sewell in his study in 1997 found that some teachers called upon racial stereotypes held within society and used these to relate to pupils. Many saw Asian pupils as being passive and conformist. One teacher from the study explained: 'Asian kids, I find them seldom in a position of conflict; they seem to have high aspirations.' In his study, in 1990, Gilborn found similar views. He noted that white teachers believed in stereotypical assumptions, that Afro-Caribbean boys represented a 'threat to authority'.

Sewell believes that, for some teachers, racism is an 'external set of beliefs that they consciously or subconsciously draw upon' in their dealings with black and Asian students (Sewell 1997: 62).

Black achievers

Not all black learners underachieve, but many report that they experienced low teacher expectation. Diane Abbott's (1989) account of how she overcame low expectation at her grammar school, applied to and gained a place at Cambridge University, reflects her courage, determination and belief in herself. She said:

I had the confidence that only unbounded ignorance can give. I had no idea what a leap it represented in class terms. In truth I had only a dim idea of how the British class systems worked, to grow up Black in Britain is to grow up an outsider and in any case, this was the sixties with its cult of egalitarianism. I did not appreciate why it should be particularly remarkable that a Black girl should go to Cambridge. I took no advice, confided in no one and, blissfully ignorant of the fact that it couldn't be done, went ahead and did it.

Case study: my experience

It is appropriate here to give my own experience as a black person who went on to achieve in the British educational system. First, I was indeed fortunate to have had my early educational experience in Jamaica, where I learnt to read and write before I went to primary school.

I came to Britain as a teenager hoping to further my education, because by this time I had become obsessed with books and learning. In Britain I soon had to find full-time employment in order to pay for basic needs like accommodation and food.

Yet I was determined to continue my education and a year later I enrolled to do eight GCEs. At first I was told I couldn't do so many, I would surely fail. I was given a test on every subject and passed before the college reluctantly enrolled me.

I attended college four evenings per week, some evenings attending two or three different classes and I was in full-time employment. I did this for two years and achieved grades A–C in all subjects. I later did two A levels in one year followed by a BA in English Literature and a PhD.

During my years of study in the education system I never had a black teacher and I saw very few in the colleges and universities that I worked or studied in. I never suffered from any direct discrimination. The teachers I met were usually indifferent; they neither encouraged nor discouraged me. Indirectly, I suffered from a Eurocentric curriculum, which ignored my culture and the benefits that BME people brought to Britain.

I was never discouraged by the low expectations that some teachers had of me because my early education was in Jamaica. I was fortunate because I did not need a black role model in Britain, because as a child I saw black people as prime ministers, judges, lawyers, doctors, teachers, engineers, artists and writers. I therefore knew that I could become what I wanted despite racism.

Underachievement in FE

As in schools, not all BME students underachieve in further education. In 1998–99 62 per cent of Caribbean students and 68.9 per cent of Indian students who finished their courses gained a qualification (CRE 2004). The question is: why did the others fail, although subjected to the same system?

The answer may lie in how individual black students react to stereotyping and low teacher expectations. Diane Abbot was carried through by ignorance of the class system and optimism. Others may have achieved because their parents were role models or they were highly motivated, confident and determined to succeed.

BME students' relationships with white teachers in FE is not as well researched as those in schools. However, colleges do have similar problems, but on a lesser scale.

Reports

The Commission for Black Staff in Further Education (2002) found that stereotyping of, particularly, Afro-Caribbean and Asian learners in colleges has a negative impact on student retention and achievement. A group of black learners told the commission about the 'rudeness and disrespect' of some staff towards 'learners whose first language was not English' and that the teaching and support they received was 'less effective, due to some tutors' low expectations' (p. 55).

Black learners

However, an LSC report, *Seeking the Views of Learners* (2001–02), found that most BME learners in FE were satisfied with the quality of teaching and training, including 56 per cent of Caribbean and 50 per cent of Indian students. But there were a significant number who were not satisfied: they said the reasons were that teachers lacked understanding of how to make subjects interesting and had poor relationships with their students.

Adult students and underachievement

BME adults are over-represented in adult learning-participation in lifelong learning:

68 per cent of people over the age of 16 participate in some form of learning. Black Africans (82 per cent) and people of 'Mixed Ethnic origin' (80 per cent) have the highest rates of participation, Black Caribbean (72 per cent), Chinese (67 per cent) and Indian (66 per cent).

(CRE 2004)

It is evident that, despite underachievement in compulsory education, BME groups regard education and training highly and are prepared to keep trying for success. Most BME adult students would have left school with few, or no qualifications and would have found that the job market had been stacked against them. All they could probably find were low-paid, low status jobs, which kept them in poverty. Having decided to do something, about their position, they returned to education to acquire the skills they needed to improve their job prospects. They have shown courage in doing so.

Difficulties

I have taught on many courses which had BME adult students. These students were usually highly motivated, bringing life and work experience to the course. However, many – usually women – were working under enormous pressure. They had domestic and childcare responsibilities, were working full time and trying to do their course work all at the same time. It is no wonder that so many underachieve or do not complete courses.

It is easy for college managers and staff to underestimate the difficulties many adult learners have to face in order to attend and finish a course. They have to juggle home and childcare responsibilities, with little if any help from partners. Many also have to cope with financial problems, because even if they have a job it is usually poorly paid.

Teachers: a guide to diversity

Teachers should:

- be given training to understand and value cultural and religious diversity as well as the needs of disabled students
- help to create an environment in the classroom and ultimately the college which is free from prejudice, discrimination and harassment
- understand the requirements of the RRAA 2000 and how they can help to promote it
- take into account students' cultural background, language needs and different styles of learning
- make sure that the curriculum they teach deals with racism and diversity
- challenge stereotypes in the curriculum, themselves and in others
- have knowledge of disadvantaged groups' social and economic history
- encourage ALL students to reach their full potential
- teach and encourage students to understand the difference in cultures and language between different ethnic groups, including white cultures
- be able to recognize racist incidents and harassment and know how to deal with them
- keep up to date with the laws on race relations and other equality legislation, and take up training opportunities
- ensure that students from all racial groups know about the different kinds of support available, for example English as a second language, study skill courses and help for childcare.

Supportive teachers

It is also important to acknowledge the many supportive teachers in FE colleges, who recognize institutional racism and its effects on society and in particular BME students in the education system. They are the ones who have argued for multicultural education for years and still are. They have supported and respected all students, including those from BME backgrounds. They have high expectations of all students, helping them to reach their full potential.

Examples of support

Talking to FE students, I heard many examples of supportive teachers. Monica, a black A level student in FE college, had nothing negative to say about her teacher, whom she felt had helped her to achieve.

I had this great teacher, he taught me sociology and from day one he helped me. He would explain things in simple language, he gave me a list of good books and feedback on my essays. Thanks to him, I got a B grade for sociology and I hope to go to university. I will never forget him.

(Ainley 1994)

Another student told me that his teacher in FE was very politically aware of racism and discrimination in education. He said he and other students liked the teacher, because she was 'fair and honest and expected the best from everyone'.

Are teachers to blame?

Anthea Davey, in her article, 'Underachievement by ethnic minority pupils should not be blamed on teachers alone', believes that too much focus has been placed on schools regarding black underachievement. She believes that children are influenced heavily by factors outside school and after all 'they spend only 15 per cent of their time in the classroom'.

Davey put forward the old simplistic theory that black underachievement cannot be caused through racism in the classroom, because children of other ethnic minority groups, such as Chinese children, achieve more over white children. Davey asked the question, if 70 per cent of black children from Caribbean families do not reach the government's landmark, what is the difference between them and the 30 per cent that do?

She argues that educational researchers and writers should also examine the influence of class and parental involvement on underachievement. She believes that the problem comes from outside the classroom, as well (Davey, *Guardian*, March 2003).

Other causes of underachievement

There are other causes for the educational underachievement of BME learners which need consideration. For example, the Runnymede Trust publication, *Black and Ethnic Minority Young People and Education Disadvantages* (2003), suggested that race couldn't be easily separated from class, when looking at educational advantages. It states, 'The influence of school is significant but social background is of much greater importance' (Runnymede Trust 2003).

Racial categorization

The Runnymede publication suggests that racial categorization is misleading, because it ignores, for instance, the social, economic and religious profile of different communities. The class theory of underachievement is backed up by reports which show the difference in ethnic minority educational achievement: they reveal that some Asian children, notably those of Chinese and Indian origin, have the best educational results:

with 73 per cent and 64 per cent respectively gaining five or more good GCSEs, ahead of white children, on 51 per cent. Bangladeshi children come some way behind that with 41 per cent, and at the bottom of the table are children of African and Pakistani origin, on 40 per cent, and Black Caribbean origin, 30 per cent.

Davey, *Guardian*, March 2003

Class

Some believe that when inequalities are looked at by race, class and gender the largest differences are found between children from middle and working-class backgrounds. The suggestion is that it is class, not race, that accounts for BME students' underachievement.

Poverty also contributes to BME student's underachievement. DfES statistics (2003) reveal that distribution figures for the Widening Participation Fund, which provide an indication of poverty, demonstrate that while 27 per cent of FE students as a whole were residents in deprived areas, 70 per cent of Bangladeshi students, 73 per cent of African students, 68 per cent of Pakistani students,

67 per cent of black Caribbean students and 64 per cent of black Other students were living in deprived areas.

Black middle class

Ethnic minority students coming from middle-class backgrounds have certain advantages that working-class students do not have. They have role models and are brought up in an atmosphere where they are expected to achieve because their parents and family have.

The 1994 study, 'Blacks and Asians in the British media', found that many black journalists went to private schools and came from homes where at least one parent had a degree and was in a managerial or professional occupation. But black parents who sent their children to private schools had not done so because they could afford it, they did so because, as one journalist explained:

I was educated at private school until I went to Cambridge and if I hadn't I would not have achieved. My parents had heard about the racist name-calling at the local school and didn't want me to go there

(Ainley 1994: 228)

Sending children back home

Another action adopted by black parents who wanted their children to succeed was to send them to the Caribbean for secondary education. Children sent to the Caribbean have several advantages, including attending a private school by day and being cared for by uncles, aunts and grandparents at night and weekends. They also 'learnt about their parents' country of origin' and 'were subjected to discipline and hard work' from black teachers who had 'high academic expectations of them' (Ainley 1994: 226)

BME parents, whether middle or working-class, value education highly and will take any action they can to help their children succeed. Those parents who cannot afford private schools send their children to supplementary or Saturday schools or pay for extra tuition.

Peer pressure

Peer pressure is another contributor to the educational under-achievement of BME students. Peer pressure usually affects young black and white males, but the effect upon young black males in schools and colleges cannot be ignored.

Tony Sewell, a higher education lecturer, studied five secondary schools in 1997 and concluded that, while 'there is a fear of Black children among some teachers', there was a bigger problem: that of 'peer group pressure and another is parental responsibility'.

For some students, peer pressure can be all-consuming, so much so that they think education is for 'sissies' and that no macho male worth his salt would be seen dead with a book. As the actor Will Smith stated about African-American maleness, 'If you don't act like an inarticulate thug you are called a "coconut" ' (Pope, *New Nation*, 18 April 2005).

The response by some young black males towards the schooling process is one of resistance. They resist because they see the process as racist and therefore feel that it has nothing to offer them. They feel alienated, not just from the education system, but from society. Their response to the education process can be that of conformity, because of the fear of unemployment, 'while others have cut out a rebel phallus that has lost touch with their minds and inner selves' (Sewell 1997: 220)

Parental responsibility

Parental responsibility is as important as teaching and learning for educational achievement. Parents are responsible for providing a learning atmosphere and encouragement for their children. If parents are role models, it is usually easier for children to achieve. Children born in families where parents are educated, well informed and take the time to teach and support children at an early age are at an advantage.

But most black parents are working-class and may not have the ability to help. They have been let down by the education system themselves. They are former underachievers, who have no confidence in themselves or a system which previously failed them and will fail their children. With no other choice, most BME parents will be hoping that educational institutions do not discriminate against their children. The best way for colleges to meet these expectations/hopes is to promote race equality through the RRAA 2000.

Black teachers

'Black teachers are in danger of becoming an endangered species' (Challender 1997)

The under-representation of black teachers in all sectors of the British education system is another reason for black underachievement. If efforts are not made by teacher training institutions to recruit and retain BME young people into the profession, then black teachers will not just be endangered, they will be wiped out.

As a result of institutional racism only a token few BME applicants are accepted on degree courses at older universities and by the Graduate Teacher Training Registry (GTTR) and the Training and Development Agency (TDA). For instance, in 1995 data published on teacher training showed that only 8 per cent of students for full-time undergraduate and sandwich courses were black.

How black teachers can help black students achieve

One way of reducing underachievement is for colleges to employ more BME teachers. They should be represented in every sector of FE, including senior management, where they are grossly underrepresented.

An effective black teacher:

- can be seen as a role model and mentor; white students and staff will be encouraged to see that BME groups are capable of achievement and this will help to challenge any stereotypes
- is able to share similar cultural backgrounds and experiences to which black students respond positively
- can instil strong and positive attitudes towards learning in black students

- can increase motivation, and promote personal and academic achievement in black learners
- has a strong attachment to the black community and feel a part of it
- has a positive perspective about African, Caribbean and Asian cultures in teaching
- regularly uses methods of teaching which draw upon cultural roots to help students succeed
- ensures that the classroom content is linked to BME student experiences and that students are encouraged to bring these into the classroom
- is concerned not only with the academic achievement of black learners, but with their social and emotional development and that this is reflected in their practice
- accepts responsibility for nurturing their students with skills necessary for success, in schools and the wider community
- encourages cultural and community teaching and learning, which goes against traditional classroom competition and individual achievement.

Creating wider subject choices

The Commission for Black Staff in Further Education found that colleges have worked hard to increase the number of learners from BME groups. Despite the increase, BME students in colleges are less likely to be studying veterinary science, or agriculture (less than 5 per cent), while representation in the following subjects is also low: education (6 per cent), humanities (6 per cent), physical sciences (under 10 per cent) and creative arts and design (under 10 per cent) (CRE 2004).

The most important reason why BME students are under-represented in some courses is racism, institutional and structural. Minorities are subjected to stereotyping by the majority and this is carried out in educational institutions. For example, in the 1960s, when thousands of Asian doctors came to Britain to work for the health service, they became synonymous with medicine and were stereotyped in this position (Ainley 1994).

Stereotyped courses

The CRE 2004 report found that 35 per cent of minority ethnic students are likely to be studying medicine or dentistry, but black Caribbean students are poorly represented at 0.3 per cent.

Some BME students get pulled into these stereotypes, feeling they will not be accepted in any other courses or job apart from the one they have been designated to by the majority, so they do not apply. This is made worse because courses such as veterinary science and agriculture have very few black staff and are usually in predominantly white colleges. It is a Catch-22 situation: if colleges do not employ black staff and do not advertise their courses in the ethnic media, then BME groups will not apply.

Non-traditional courses

An important question for BME young people who want to enter a non-stereotypical course is, will they get a job after the course? The answer is yes, but probably only after a lot of rejection. However, this should not stop BME students from applying for non-traditional courses, even though at present the job market is discriminatory; just because the door is now only half open, it does not mean it cannot be fully opened.

How colleges can create wider subject choices

- Advertise courses widely in the local community and BME media.
- On courses where BME students are underrepresented, advertisements should state that they are welcome to apply.
- College careers advisors should encourage BME students towards non-traditional courses, such as science, humanities and creative courses such as art and design.
- Colleges could send tutors and students, including those from BME groups, to schools and community centres to market these courses to underrepresented groups, encouraging them to apply.
- The presence of BME teachers on non-traditional courses will encourage more black students.

- By getting involved in courses such as applied science for medicine, dentistry and medical sciences, e.g. LOCN access courses to higher education. These courses help mature students, those on low income and especially students from Afro-Caribbean backgrounds, who are underrepresented on these courses, to get the opportunity to study medicine and science.

Model college policy for diversity

- A place on the right course
- Impartial advice and information
- Expert induction and teaching
- Regular tutorials to review progress
- High-quality learning resources
- Friendly and helpful staff
- A supportive and secular college environment
- A voice in the way the college is run
- A quick and positive response to complaints and suggestions
- Firm action on any harassment or bad behaviour
- A curriculum which values and recognizes the achievement of different cultures, races and religions
- A racial equality policy which promotes good relations between students and staff of different races
- An equal representation of BME staff in all sectors of the college
- Clear and correct information and advice about course fees, grants, childcare, accommodation and state benefits
- A clear learning agreement, setting out your learning goals
- A student handbook which details the college services and information about students' rights and responsibilities
- An assessment of language and numerical skills and, if appropriate, specialist help given
- Support from tutors while on placement
- Firm action on racial discrimination in colleges or on work placement.

Monitoring

The RRAA 2000 asks colleges to monitor by racial groups the admission and progress of students.

Monitoring is the collection of information to see whether an institution's policies and practices are helping to achieve race equality for students and staff in order to assess the situation properly.

Students

Data required for monitoring student admission include:

- applications
- choice of subjects
- achievement and retention
- student residential status – e.g. home or international
- where overseas students are recruited
- information as to how many home or international students are accepted
- a breakdown of applications, showing the number of ethnic minority applications to each subject
- data about each student's age, gender, disability status and ethnic origin
- information about students accepting places, selection methods and formal and informal interviews.

Admission criteria

Admission criteria should be clear to everyone, especially staff who are responsible for applications and the admission of students. It is important to monitor whether the admission process is based on equality and diversity.

It is also important to establish, if appropriate, the reasons why students from some ethnic minority groups are underrepresented on certain courses, or do not apply. To gain this information, colleges may have to consult young people from the concerned group, including those students attending the college. Data can also be collected from the CRE, local equality groups, student unions and national surveys.

Assessment

The assessment may find that the college needs to revise its admission practices and policies in order to promote equality. Targets should be set and monitoring procedures and practices drawn up in order to improve BME student retention and achievement rates within the college especially on courses in which they are underrepresented.

The revised policies and procedures should be communicated to all staff and student organizations and publicized in the college newsletter, website, student unions and on college noticeboards.

Student retention

To assess why students are dropping out of courses colleges need to monitor:

- the number of students dropping out, according to racial group
- which courses are being left
- reasons for leaving
- information on departmental and subject drop-out rates

The college may need to monitor its services aimed at supporting students. Information should be collected on levels of satisfaction and the appropriateness of the service provided in response to the needs of students. After the assessment has been carried out and the main reasons for students dropping out have been established, the college will have to change its policies, either partly or fully, so as to improve retention rates. Whatever changers are made, staff and student representatives, equal opportunity groups, governors and black focus groups should be informed.

Student achievement

As part of the duty to promote race equality, colleges are obliged to monitor and assess the levels of achievement for students from different ethnic backgrounds. The areas which must be monitored and assessed include:

- monitoring student numbers, transfers and drop-out rates
- difference in methods of assessment

- work placements
- jobs arising from work placements
- the result of programmes targeted at people from specific racial groups
- language support for BME students
- reported incidents of racial discrimination and outcomes of any investigations
- teaching and learning support
- curriculum and diversity
- issues regarding student expulsion.

Colleges are required to assess their policies to see if they affect students from a variety of ethnic backgrounds differently. They should consult student and staff union representatives and any support groups that represent minority groups. Colleges could set up focus groups to investigate any complaints or issues facing students and their achievements.

If policies are not working, they will need to be revised and colleges should put into place strategies which will help to promote race equality. For example, teaching, learning and the curriculum should be examined carefully to see if they embody race equality and diversity.

Student experience

The college's policy on bullying and harassment should cover all staff and students. In assessing how well the policy is working, colleges should monitor by ethnicity all forms of complaints from students, including racial harassment and bullying. The complaint may be from one student about another student or about staff, teaching and non-teaching. Anonymous questionnaires may be given to students, past and present, in order to get the information needed.

If, after assessment, the college finds that its bullying and harassment policy is not working, it will have to revise all or part of it. Questions which should be asked include:

- are complaints about racism ignored and not taken seriously?
- are complaints being investigated within a reasonable period of time?
- are students making complaints labelled as troublemakers?

Teaching and learning support

Monitoring should include student experiences in teaching, learning and the curriculum. It should look at how students are assessed, academic support and other student support facilities. The curriculum content is particularly important to BME students and should be monitored and assessed. For instance, does the curriciculum:

- value and recognize the achievements of different cultures and religions?
- promote racial equality through its contents, or is it mainly monocultural, promoting Eurocentric values, while ignoring other cultures?

And does the college:

- have black role models in the form of lecturers and senior managers, or is there an underrepresentation of BME staff, especially in senior positions? If this is the case, then the college will have to introduce race employment targeting and other positive action policies, such as mentoring and work shadowing
- have policies and practices that challenge stereotype? For example, does the college typecast Afro-Caribbean males as confrontational and aggressive and Asians as conformist?
- have teaching staff who encourage all students to achieve their full potential?
- give all students the same support, or do they expect some groups to fail?

Expulsion

Colleges should not use expulsion as the only disciplinary measure for students who do not fall into line. It is important that the policies and procedures in relation to expulsion are monitored by ethnicity, and that students who have been expelled are interviewed. If assessment finds that black students, for instance, are being expelled disproportionately, then serious consideration must be given to whether institutional racism and stereotyping is at work and what action needs to be taken to reduce the number of expulsions.

Serious action

While most colleges are in the business of keeping students because of the financial implications, there are others who are still expelling young black men (The Commission for Black Staff 2002). Expulsion is a very serious action and should not be taken lightly. Colleges should be willing to take advice from outside agencies such as the CRE and LSC. If found to be discriminating, colleges may find themselves facing legal actions and negative publicity and, if found guilty, a large fine. The implications of expelling young people from education institutions have far-reaching consequences. Such action may jeopardize the future of that young person and their family for life.

Case study 1

After monitoring and assessment, a college found that Afro-Caribbean students were overrepresented in certain vocational courses and underrepresented in courses such as science, maths, education studies and humanities.

Further investigation was carried out and questionnaires given to students, past and present. The college found that Afro-Caribbean students did not apply for certain courses because they did not know about them and had low aspirations, and the college did not have many black teachers and so very few role models.

As a result the college publicized all its courses through the ethnic media, local papers and community organizations. Publicity was also modified to include images that represented the ethnic diversity of students and staff.

In addition, the college set up a working group of staff and students, including BME students, to determine what action should be taken to get information to its target audience. The working group met with local community religious institutions and consulted with young people about the college courses offered. They explained the advantage for BME students in undertaking courses such as science, maths and languages.

In the first year after this positive action the intake of BME learners onto science and maths courses rose by 10 per cent.

Case study 2

A college running a course in veterinary science sent six students on work placement to a farm it had used for several years. The group of six, including one black student, were given duties each day by the farmer and supervised. However, as the days went by, the farmer began to supervise the Black student less and less, until eventually he stopped speaking to her.

Lost, hurt and with nothing to do, she followed and shadowed the rest of the group. Eventually, she reported the farmer to her college.

As a result, the college sent out a standard contract to every work-placement provider. The contract set out what the college expected from the provider, in terms of equal opportunity, as well as the standard support all students should receive throughout their placement.

The college decided that it would not use employers who failed to meet these standards, or who had no equal opportunity policy for their own staff. It increased the numbers of course tutors, which would ensure that students on placements got adequate support, with regular contact with students and providers to discuss student progress. As a result of this experience, the college has offered race equality training for all of its placement providers.

Case study 3

A college, alarmed by the number of ethnic minority students dropping out, monitored its race policies and practices. It found that students dropping out were those to whom

English was a second language (ESOL). Further investigation was carried out and questionnaires were sent to current students and those who had left. Results showed that students left because they were not able to cope with the course, and that the language support courses, which had been set up at the college, were not working effectively.

As a result, the college increased and improved its language support services, employing more language specialist teachers. It also made sure that all ESOL students were offered language support at registration and that their progress reviewed each term.

Summary

Here we looked at black students' educational underachievement and why it occurred. We found that the two most important causes were racism and stereotyping. Black students in FE and the British education system in general have a problematic relationship with some white teachers, who see them as being a threat to authority.

This chapter also examines the role that black teachers could have on the educational achievement of black students, if they were employed in sufficient numbers in FE.

We also look at how colleges can create wider subject choices for BME students and how to get more into courses where they are underrepresented in order to promote race equality. This chapter also gives practical guides on how colleges should monitor and assess student admission, retention, achievement, teaching and learning support.

4 Multicultural education

Curriculum

The first step towards a multicultural curriculum process is to examine the biases, prejudices and assumptions that are carried by society and textbooks about 'the other'. Teachers must always examine the contents of the curriculum for prejudice and negative images of BME groups.

Eurocentric curriculum

Many people, including teachers, accept the present curriculum as normal, without question, while others see it as racist, sexist, classist and white male orientated. The present curriculum is mostly geared to a white, Christian population. Despite the RRAA 2000, the curriculum in schools, colleges and higher education institutions is still Euro and male-centric, both in content and perspective. It virtually ignores the history of women and BME groups.

Such biased information is misleading to students and reinforces a false sense of superiority by the dominant group, while denying the contributions to world development by less dominant groups (see, for example, www.edchange.org/multicultural/curriculum/setps.html, 14 November 2005)

Resisting change

The introduction of the RRAA 2000 gives the best opportunity to bring about change. The curriculum must become more inclusive, if the British education system is serious about race equality.

The present Eurocentric curriculum is partly responsible for the underachievement of black learners in education. Yet there is still resistance by some colleges to multicultural education. One black learner summed up the curriculum found in many colleges and higher education institutions by saying: 'I used to write down all this stuff about kings and queens and all the European history because I wanted to get through. There was nothing about Asian or black history. It is as if we didn't exist' (Mac an Ghaill 1988: 282).

Attacks on all fronts

The idea of a multicultural curriculum was attacked on all fronts. The right saw it as an 'attempt to politicise education in order to pander to minority demands', which would be harmful to pupils and would threaten British culture (Scruton 1986: 37).

Some writers argued that multicultural education was inhibited, because there was a general confusion about the term and how it should be integrated and taught. Cohen and Manion (1983) made it clear in their description what a multicultural curriculum is. It is:

one in which choice of contents reflects the multicultural nature of British Society and the world, and draws significantly on the experiences of British Racial Minorities and overseas cultures.

(Cohen and Manion 1983: 118)

Multicultural education

The problem is that BME cultures are judged against British and western cultures, when there is no need, as each culture has its own validity. Although the DfES gave its support in the 1980s to multicultural education, it has failed to give clear leadership on this subsequently. As a result, the concept of a multicultural curriculum has become a piecemeal affair, with schools and colleges making up their own policies as they went along, without much success.

The RRAA 2000, if implemented by colleges, should stop the confusion, as it gives clear and practical advice on how educational institutions can make the curriculum inclusive.

Black studies

Another aspect of multicultural education introduced in the 1970s was black studies. The concept came from the Black Power Movement in the USA. These courses were mainly taught by black teachers and were aimed at Afro-Caribbean pupils who were said to have low self-esteem and had lost their sense of identity:

- black studies popularized the concept of affirmative action
- it sought to redress the historical imbalance by teaching about black history and culture and its contribution to the world
- it explains the struggles past and present against racism and inequality
- it provides a black perspective for the curriculum as opposed to a white western one
- it encourages black students to be proud of their past and present, which in turns helps to boost the confidence of black learners who may have low self-esteem due to a racist curriculum.

Women's studies

Like black studies it is important to have women's studies in colleges and universities but, unlike black studies, women's studies have been established in several universities around the world, especially in Europe and the USA.

The feminist movement has a long history of campaigning for change. It has improved the situation for women, including voting rights, the rights to stand for political office, greater access to education, employment and birth control. However, this is only a partial success because many inequalities still remain between men and women. Despite this, women have seen much more progress against sexual discrimination than black people have seen against racism.

How FE managers can change the curriculum

What can managers of further education do to make changes in the curriculum so as to incorporate the cultural diversity of their students and staff? Managers should ensure that:

- the curriculum is continually audited
- the contents of the curriculum are reviewed to see if they are free of racial bias
- space is given to equality issues
- departments monitor and assess their curriculum to see if it meets the needs of all its students
- the curriculum is planned so it represents other cultures.
- race equality and diversity is built into all teaching and learning policies and practices
- time and resources are available for multicultural teaching.

Facts for multicultural teaching

A multicultural curriculum should include the fact that African, Caribbean and Asian people didn't first come to Britain after the war. In fact, the black presence in Britain first began in AD 208 when the Roman Emperor Septimius Severus marched to northern Britain to complete its conquest. Mission unaccomplished, he died (aged 65) at York in 211. He was an African from Leptis Magna on the North Coast of the Continent. Since 1555 there has been a permanent black presence in England, which has been ignored (Fryer 1984: 1).

It might not be generally known that many rich families in Britain had black servants and that there were also thousands of free black people in major cities in the UK, including Cardiff and Liverpool. Black communities have been in these areas for many generations. Although the majority of black people during the seventeenth and eighteenth century were as poor as their white neighbours, some did manage to move out of poverty, prospered and contributed to every aspect of British life.

The black presence in Britain

How many students or staff in colleges or higher education institutions know the extent of the contribution that BME groups made during the world wars? In the First World War 1.5 million Indians were enlisted and 40,000 were killed.

Similarly, thousands of Africans and Caribbeans enlisted and many were killed. The Second World War also brought thousands of African, Caribbean and Asian people to Britain in order to fight for 'king and country'. They joined the forces and worked in munitions factories. The largest volunteer army in history came from India, with 2.5 million Indian people fighting.

It is only recently that the BME contributions to this major part of European history have been recognized. Countless films, books and articles have been published about the world wars, yet the black contribution has been rarely acknowledged. None of the black people who were in the First or Second World Wars are famous, but they have helped achieve the freedom of Europe. They are the forgotten heroes of multicultural Britain.

Prosperous Africans and Caribbeans

- Mary Seacole was a Jamaican nurse and a 'born healer' who challenged society to put her skills to proper use, despite being black. She side-stepped official indifference and paid her way to the Crimea, where she worked with wounded and dying soldiers. She was the first black woman to make a mark on British public life. However, while Florence Nightingale was turned into a heroine, Mary Seacole was relegated into obscurity and only recently rescued.
- William Cuffay was born in Chatham in 1788. He was a tailor and one of the leaders and martyrs of the Chartist movement, the first mass political movement of the British working class. His grandfather was an African who was sold into slavery on the island of St Kitts, where his father was born a slave. In 1848 he was put on trial for levying war against Queen Victoria and at the age of 61 was transported for life to Tasmania.
- Samuel Coleridge Taylor was born in Holborn in 1875. He

made one of the biggest contributions by a black person to British concert music. He integrated traditional black music into concert music. He wrote many compositions, including African Romances, 1897; African Suite, 1898 and Overture to the song of Hiawatha, 1899. The first performance of his Hiawatha's Wedding Feast, 1889, was described by the principal of the Royal College of Music as one of the most remarkable events in modern English musical history (Fryer 1984: 256).

Prosperous Asians

- Sake Deen Mahomed, an Indian from Patna, who had been employed as a surgeon, arrived in Cork in the late eighteenth century. He married an Irish girl and moved to Brighton, where the two set up a business called Mahomed Baths. Mahomed had long been interested in steam baths and massage as a cure for various ailments. He successfully proved the value of his treatments and had many illustrious patrons including George IV, who made Mahomed the Superintendent of his baths at Brighton Pavilion.
- The first Asian in Britain to engage in any kind of political activity was Raja Rammohan Roy, who was here from 1830 to 1833. Poet, philosopher, reformer and journalist, he was the first Brahman to visit London. During his stay, Roy submitted to the parliamentary committee on Indian Affairs a memorandum, which was the first authentic statement of Indian views placed before the British authorities by an eminent Indian.
- Dadabhai Naoroji was born in Bombay in 1825, the son of a Parsee priest. At the age of 29, he became the first Indian Professor of Mathematics and Natural Philosophy. He came to Britain in 1855 and was appointed Professor of

> Gujerati at University College London in 1859. He was
> the first Asian to be elected to the House of Commons in
> 1896.

Science in a multicultural curriculum

The questions and discussions which should be addressed by college managers and lecturers in introducing a multicultural science
curriculum are:

- what is science?
- is it part of western culture or is it universal?
- does science have a role in anti-racist teaching?
- do science teachers have a responsibility to teach from a
  multicultural perspective as part of the college's race equality
  policy?
- are science teachers aware of the possible areas of conflict
  between the religious beliefs of their students and the content
  of their science classes?

Resources

College managers and science teachers should make sure that:

- science materials are not biased
- images of BME groups are not portrayed negatively
- science materials reflect the work of third-world scientists and
  that their work is given equal value and significance to that of
  western scientists.

Some science teachers still find it difficult to accept that science
can be multicultural. They see the subject as colour-blind, neutral
or objective, although some textbooks from the 1970s have tried to
take into account the historical and cultural diversity of science.
Newnham and Watts (1984) demonstrated the universal development of science, stressing the African contribution. Also in *Black
Scientists and Inventions* (1998), it was shown how the black contribution to science has been ignored. It also looked at the history of
chemistry and showed that it contained worldwide contributions,
challenging the view that chemistry was a European convention.

In order to dispel these myths, teachers must:

- inform themselves about the history of science and the contributions of non-European countries and pass this knowledge on to students
- initiate discussions and debate. Through this students' knowledge will be enhanced, enabling them to gain a better understanding of science as a diverse and global subject
- teach students to understand science as a universal subject developed through worldwide contributions derived from people of all races, religions and colours.

This will help to dispel the racist stereotypical images found in some science textbooks and materials. A number of black scientists have contributed to science, but much of their work has been largely ignored. Here are a few of these scientists.

Black pioneers of science

- Dr Mae Jemison developed a health care programme for volunteers in the Peace Corps and personnel of the US State department. She also worked as a doctor in Los Angeles. The talented Dr Jemison received the 1988 Essences Science and Technology award and also had the honour of being selected from over 2,000 applicants to participate in an astronaut-training program at NASA. She was the first black woman in space.
- Professor Charles Ssali is an African doctor/scientist who was born in Uganda. In 1992 he invented a treatment for HIV/Aids called Mariandiana A, B, J, for which he obtained a British patent (patent no. 2224649). This treatment involves taking a course of pills fortified with 100 per cent natural ingredients. He is presently the director of Mariandiana Aids Research Foundation. Professor Charles Ssali is hailed as a national hero of the Ugandan people.
- Garret A. Morgan was an African who had only an elementary school education. Garrett invented the first gas mask in 1912 and was given a patent for it by the US government. Subsequently, Garret received very large contracts

from all around the country to supply his gas mask to fire departments, mining companies and the US army. In 1923 Garret Morgan received a patent for the invention of a traffic signalling system. Before his invention there were many street accidents. Later on, Morgan sold the rights to General Electric Corporation for $40,000.

Examples for multicultural science teaching

- T. Elkins – patented the chamber commode in 1872
- T. J. Martin – patented the fire extinguisher in 1872
- E. McCoy – patented the steam lubricator in 1874
- L. H. Latimer – patented an apparatus for cooling and disinfecting in 1886
- A. B. Blackburn – patented the railway signal in 1888
- W. B. Purvis – patented the fountain pen in 1890
- Granville T. Woods – patented the safety cut-out for electric circuits in 1891
- Bassie Coleman, born 1893 – the first African American woman aviator
- M. A. Cherry – patented the streetcar fender in 1895
- W. H. Jackson – patented a railway switch in 1898
- J. H. Robinson – patented life-saving guards for locomotives in 1899
- S. W. Gunn – patented a shoe in 1900
- P. B. Williams – patented an electrically controlled and operated railway in 1901
- A. D. Washington – patented a shoehorn in 1903
- Granville T. Woods – patented an electric railway system in 1903

Multicultural mathematics

Mathematics has traditionally been seen as an isolated subject 'linked to sciences via calculations and manipulations of formulae' (Newnham and Watts 1984: 97). It is linked to the social sciences for statistics and analysis. Mathematics teaching, like science teaching, traditionally perpetuated the idea of the European or North American white male as the most important contributor to the subject. Mathematics is, however, open to a multicultural approach and cultural differences can improve the quality of mathematic experiences and challenge the idea of European and North American superiority.

Managers and teachers in colleges should include in mathematic teaching:

- a history of the subject that clearly shows the contributions of a number of cultures and from a wider diversity of people
- the historical debt to Eastern Cultures for systems of representation, including the Arabic derivation of algebra (*al-jabr*) and spatial geometric imagery, both of which form a basis for mathematical understand in all cultures
- the African Mende addition, a method of addition used by the Mende people of West Africa. This method uses counting and expansions to build towards the idea of addition. Mathematics is part of the Mende traditional culture. Mende addition can be used in basic skills, mathematics, pre-algebra and algebra courses (see: www.deltncollege.edu/dept/basicmath/mende.-htm).

Exploring immigration and racism through literature

As an English literature teacher in FE I was able to explore social and political issues in the curriculum without much difficulty. I started off with nothing but the commitment to make the curriculum multicultural. Here is an example.

A study of immigration to Britain

Over 50 per cent of those I taught were either immigrants or children of immigrants. I introduced the subject by giving handouts which contained factual information such as information about the first 500 immigrants to post-war Britain who arrived in 1948 on SS *Empire Windrush* from Jamaica.

- This was followed by a general discussion on immigration and racism.
- The class was broken up into pairs and students were asked to list questions that they wished to ask each other about immigration and assimilation.
- Interviews were carried out over two lessons. For homework students were asked to interview their parents and other family members who had immigrated to Britain.
- Native students were also involved but they were paired with a BME student who had an immigrant background. They could list and ask questions on immigrations. There was also a white South African student and a Scottish student who talked about their own cultures and their experiences on immigrating to London.
- After the interviews were concluded, the class came back together to share what they had learnt from each other and their own personal experiences. Students did not have to share these experiences unless they wanted to, but everyone wanted to be involved.

Topics covered
- immigrants' country of origin
- what these countries were like
- why people immigrated
- did students or their parents have to learn English?
- do they still speak in their native language?
- did they experience prejudice and hostility as immigrants or as a member of a BME group?
- do they still observe customs from their country of origin and why?
- what is the best thing about living in Britain?
- what is the worst thing about living in Britain?
- write an essay on immigration to Britain.

What students gained

- more knowledge about themselves and their histories, which is not usually acknowledge in the curriculum or the media
- the opportunity to explore the issues of multicultural Britain and learn about different cultures and customs
- skills on listening, speaking, note-taking and writing essays
- the opportunity to learn about complex issues of immigration

Multicultural geography

Geography, like all other subjects, should be presented from a variety of perspectives. Teachers should:

- examine textbooks for negative images of non-European groups
- show the interdependence of countries for materials and goods
- explore the negative effects of western influence on third world development
- challenge the idea that poor countries are responsible for their poverty and instead look at the political and economic aspects of their problems
- explain and explore the issues of immigration, which is presented as a problem in many textbooks about geography. Instead teachers should look at why people immigrate and the prejudices and hostility they face.

Teaching multicultural education

The opportunity to challenge racism and to promote cultural diversity in education depend upon those who manage and teach the curriculum and their commitment to the race equality process. If teachers are to be effective, they need to be working in an environment in which racism is acknowledged and challenged. Managers of colleges and higher education institutions should create such an atmosphere by:

actively promoting Race equality and good race relations ... and be

responsible and accountable for implementing the Race equality policy and procedure.

(*Summary Report of the Commission for Black Staff in Further Education* 2002)

In an educational institution which is committed to racial equality; teachers should have the opportunity to be engaged in the development and changing of the curriculum for the benefit of all groups of learners. However, to do so effectively, teachers must have knowledge of race equality and diversity. Is initial teacher training preparing teachers for this task?

Teacher training

It would be difficult for teacher training to teach everything that new teachers need to know about teaching and equal opportunities in three years, let alone the one year that the PGCE takes. What is important, however, is that students' teachers are at least aware of the need for racial equality in every aspect of the education system. It should also be stressed that they as individuals have a responsibility to treat all learners equally and help them to fulfil their potential. Student teachers need to understand structural inequality and be prepared to deal with equality issues in schools and colleges in order to meet the needs of all their pupils.

Student teachers

Managers need to understand and accept the existence of institutional racism in education and the need to educate and prepare student teachers to teach in a multicultural society. BME student teachers will be vulnerable to racism in teacher training as well as in the classroom. They should be prepared to deal with ways in which to respond to discrimination and should be aware of the college's race equality policy on racial harassment and bullying. Managers should make it clear that racial discrimination is not tolerated.

Case history

The college did an audit of the curriculum and found that none of the courses, except one, health and social care, was doing anything to include diversity in the curriculum

A meeting was called by the Race/Equality manager with the principal and members of the senior management team. There were also representatives from staff and student unions, equal opportunity and black focus groups.

The issues of why the curriculum had to include diversity and how it should be done were discussed. As a result a curriculum group was formed which was responsible for collecting information that could be used to make the curriculum more diverse. They sought help from the CRE, staff unions and other colleges which had introduced diversity into their curricula.

The group made sure that all managers and teachers had race and diversity training and knew how to make the curriculum more multicultural without too much trouble.

Summary

In this chapter we examined the present Eurocentric curriculum that still continues in many FE colleges. We argued that colleges should move towards a more inclusive curriculum, one which represents different countries and cultures.

It is neither acceptable nor tenable for colleges to accept without question a curriculum which is geared to a mostly white male and Christian population, when Britain is multicultural and multiracial.

This chapter gives practical advice and guidance to managers and lecturers on how they can change the curriculum from Eurocentric to multicultural.

5 Recruiting and retention of BME staff

Black principals

In 2002 the Commission for Black Staff in Further Education found that there were only four black principals within mainstream colleges, constituting less than 1 per cent. At the managerial level, black staff constituted 4.9 per cent of managers, 3.8 per cent of heads of departments, 4.9 per cent of senior lecturers and 6.9 per cent of main grade lecturers.

In 2005 the number of black principals within further education rose to seven. Although changing in the right direction, at this pace it will be a long time before race equality is achieved. Some colleges use the national figure of 8.9 per cent for BME groups in Britain as a benchmark.

Benchmark

However, the benchmark which colleges should in fact be using is the student population. In London the BME groups make up 39 per cent of the student population in further education, followed by the West Midlands with 15.6 per cent and the East Midlands with 12.9 per cent (CRE 2004). The BTEG survey *Race Equality Work in Further Education Colleges* (2005) found that 'average proportions of Black staff in colleges is lower than the average proportion of Black students' (p. 19).

Better qualified

Some colleges argue that underrepresentation is due to BME staff not applying for jobs, or because they did not have the qualifications or experience. The view that BME groups do not have qualifications or experience for jobs in further education is used as an excuse for continuing racial inequality. The fact is BME groups are more qualified than their white colleagues. The Commission for Black Staff in Further Education (2002) found 'that 55 per cent of Black staff have been educated to first-degree level compared to 49 per cent of white staff and only 6 per cent of Black staff have no formal qualifications compared to 8 per cent of white staff' (p. 7).

Underrepresentation

Why is there an underrepresentation of BME lecturers, managers and principals in further education, when there are pages of vacancies advertised weekly in national newspapers? Institutional racism, stereotyping and the educational underachievement of black learners are all part of the problem. BME staff, especially those in senior positions, will continue to be underrepresented if colleges fail to promote race equality.

The report

The Black Training and Enterprise Groups' (BTEG) 2005 survey found that, while a number of colleges appear to be making good progress in meeting the RRAA in some areas, little or no progress is being made in others. These include the setting of race equality employment targets: only 20 per cent of colleges were doing this and '44 per cent reported that they had no plans to do so'. The second area of concern was that colleges were not reflecting ethnic diversity on their corporation board, with '30 per cent of colleges having no Black governors'.

Reasons for underrepresentation of BME teachers in FE include colleges:

- not making race equality issues a priority, and adopting a colour-blind attitude
- refusing to accept that their policies and practices are discriminatory against BME staff and learners
- refusing to set race equality employment targets
- not reflecting ethnic diversity on their corporation board
- not reflecting diversity in management

- having a poor record on career development and promotion of BME staff
- turning a blind eye to racial harassment and bullying.

Informal recruitment

One unfair practice still carried out in some colleges is that of word-of-mouth recruitment. Colleges are not the only institutions involved in this form of recruitment. In the media, for example, it is generally accepted that jobs depend upon whom you know (Ainley 1998). The Commission for Black Staff in FE found word of mouth recruitment in all sectors of further education colleges. It was most problematic in part-time appointments, where key posts were identified for people who had been 'ring-fenced' and encouraged to apply and get appointed. The report also found that only 42 per cent of colleges surveyed used formal recruitment procedures when appointing part-time staff.

In many cases jobs went to family members and those politically aligned with management. BME individuals are rarely part of this group, in which friendships and alliances are formed through a pub and barbecue culture, and therefore BME groups are not considered for jobs, despite their qualifications and experience.

Indirect discrimination

Although there is no deliberate intention to exclude BME groups from getting jobs, informal recruitment does have that effect. In this form of recruitment, the best person does not necessarily get the job. It is unfair on students, colleges and staff who apply formally to get their jobs. 'Word of mouth' recruitment makes a mockery of race equality policies and is illegal.

Black staff told the commission that informal recruitment practices had a negative impact on their career progression. Many trying to get permanent positions found that informal recruitment procedures were being used, even when this was not within college policy.

How FE can attract BME staff

- Advertise all jobs internally and externally unless there are special circumstances when this is not possible.
- Jobs should be advertised in national and ethnic media.
- Advertising jobs in ethnic media is seen as a genuine appeal for BME applicants.
- Colleges who advertise only in national papers are indirectly discriminating against BME groups. Adverts in national papers are not accessible to a significant number of people from underrepresented groups, so therefore they are unable to apply for jobs.
- Adverts should make it clear that underrepresented groups such as BME and disabled peopled are 'welcome' to apply.

Examples of positive adverts to attract a diversity of applications

- 'We are an equal opportunities employer and welcome applications from all sections of the community, whilst affirming that appointment will be strictly upon merit.'
- '. . . an equal opportunities employer and seeks to reflect the diverse community that it serves. Applications are welcome from anyone who meets the stated requirements.'
- 'We particularly welcome female applications and those from an Ethnic Minority, as they are underrepresented . . . at this level. This is in line with section 48 of the Sex Discrimination Act and section 38 of the Race Relations Act.'

(The Times Higher Educational Supplement
5 April 2005)

Positive images

As part of its race equality policy the college should promote positive images of BME staff and students. The purpose is to convey the message of the college's equality and diversity values.

- These images should be placed in reception areas, the first access point of the college, where internal and external customers can see them. All staff working in these areas should be well aware of their responsibility to equality and diversity.

- Positive images can be provided through posters and photographs demonstrating the college's diversity of students and staff. Photographs of governors, including BME governors, should also be placed in reception areas, with names and contact numbers.
- The college's race equality policy, notices and course information should be printed in the relevant community languages. Images used should reflect students and staff, past and present, studying or working in non-stereotyped activities.
- Colleges should promote and celebrate diversity by giving notice of events like Black History Month, Diwali, Eid and the achievements of all learners, including BME learners.

Targeting black staff

The setting of race employment targets in colleges is a piecemeal affair. The Black Training and Enterprise Group Survey (2005) found that most colleges were not setting targets and the reasons given were:

- college data management systems need to be improved before targets can be set and monitored
- college principals and/or governors are opposed to target setting
- there is no need to set targets, as the staff and student profiles are already representative of the local community
- there is no point in setting targets because they won't be achieved.

(*Race Equality Work in Further Education Colleges* 2005)

Opposing targets

Frankly, these are excuses by colleges not to set race equality employment targets. They have had enough time to improve their data systems since the RRAA 2000 became law in 2002. Principals and governors who oppose setting targets can become a serious obstacle to the implementation of race equality in their college.

They should be required to take training and have their responsibilities for implementing the RRAA 2000 made clear.

Why targeting is important
Targets will provide colleges with direction and motivation in challenging race inequality. This is positive action which gives a clear commitment to achieving a more diverse and representative workforce.

Target-setting should be central to all the college's planning and review strategies. For target-setting to work, all staff and stakeholders should be involved and the reasons for implementation communicated. This information will help to motivate heads of departments and other senior staff who are responsible for the process. However, it is not enough just to talk about setting targets: it has to be put into practice and reviewed. Putting targeting into practice is challenging, especially in colleges where governors and senior managers are resistant or have little or no knowledge about the implications of racism in the educational system and society.

What is needed to make target-setting successful in the long term is:

- an action plan which makes clear individual responsibilities and timetables
- a list of priorities agreed with managers, unions and other senior staff
- revision of policies and practices which discriminate
- consultation of data from management, CRE, staff unions and national surveys
- race equality and management training for all involved in the process
- consultation with target groups explaining the process of targeting and why they are chosen
- regular review of the process against targets and if necessary changes in policy to reach targets
- progression reports for governors, staff union representatives and other relevant key staff.

(The Commission for Black Staff in Further Education,
Race Equality in Further Education Colleges 2003a)

Ethnic monitoring

Before colleges can use targets effectively, they have to monitor the admission, recruitment and progression of staff from all racial groups. Monitoring will help colleges examine the representation of racial groups within their workforce. It will help to highlight any inequalities and offer colleges the opportunity to investigate the cause and remove any practices or policies that are unfair.

Ethnic monitoring of college recruitment procedures is vital in order to increase the numbers of black staff.

Data required in the monitoring of staff recruitment include:

- selecting and training panel members
- applications
- invitation to interviews
- success rates for different selection methods
- permanent, temporary or fixed-term appointments
- level of success by position, e.g. permanent, fixed-term, fulltime, part-time, casual, hourly paid
- home or international status.

Data required to monitor staff career progression include:

- staff grade and type of post held
- staff length of service
- staff training and development
- the progress of different racial groups
- the result of training and career development programmes or strategies that target staff from particular racial groups.

Using data from monitoring

Using the data collected from monitoring, colleges will have solid information to act on rather than basing actions on guesswork or assumptions. For example, if a college decides to increase the number of BME teachers employed, it should use monitoring data to assess why the college is currently lacking BME staff and use this information to reduce the underrepresentation.

This information should also be used to see where in the recruitment system BME groups are being rejected. If the reason for underrepresentation is that applications from ethnic minorities are not accepted, then there is no point in advertising jobs in the ethnic media, as the problem lies within the recruitment policies and procedures themselves.

Without ethnic monitoring and race employment targets, staff and learners will see the institution's race equality policy as simply paying lip service to the problem and the college will lose credibility.

Talent in diversity

Ethnic monitoring can help colleges recognize the multitude of talent that they have available, both within the diverse workforce and outside of the college. It will also help to identify the barriers that are preventing colleges from benefiting from the skills offered by a diverse workforce.

Monitoring will also prevent colleges from costly legal action, that could be bought by individuals with complaints of discrimination. Ethnic monitoring and race equality targets will also help to promote the college itself as a good and fair employer and provider of educational services.

Retention of black staff

Monitoring will help colleges to understand why they are unable to retain BME staff. There are many issues surrounding retention, the main one being institutional racism. 'Ghettoisation' is another reason why people leave.

Ghettoization

Many black staff are limited to certain subject areas, such as 'continuing education', where they teach basic English, or those for whom English is a second language. While these are important subjects, very few black lecturers get the opportunity to teach mathematics, science and literature.

Some colleges undervalue BME lecturers along with the subjects they teach and, as a result, they are not usually considered for promotion. Lack of promotion and not having the opportunity for career development are other important reasons why black staff leave.

Colleges without a race equality policy and those that have one but are not promoting it will be more vulnerable to the continued practice of institutional racism. If the race equality policies of colleges are not being implemented, or if they are ineffective, it is not difficult to see why black staff are leaving.

BME part-time staff

Many BME staff do not become part-time out of choice. They are forced to take these positions because it is better than no job at all. I have met several part-time BME teachers in colleges, teaching Basic English, who have two or three degrees, including PhDs.

These lecturers work part-time, with the hope of getting the opportunity for career development and promotion, but after many years of working and waiting nothing happens and they leave.

Although not all part-time BME lecturers want full-time jobs and promotion, they still want to be appreciated and colleges should try to retain them. They should be given equal access to training and re-training and to full-time jobs and promotion.

Support groups

Mentoring schemes should be set up, along with support groups to help with the recruitment and retention of BME staff. These groups will have a common interest and can be an important tool for empowering minorities. They can also serve as a support network and provide a means of communication between an organization, its staff and the community. These groups should provide a forum for the following:

- identifying shared issues, views and concerns
- exploring strategies for improving access and participation
- verifying findings, perceptions or assumptions
- consultation
- review of relevant policies
- scrutiny of ethnic data, benchmarks and targets
- impact assessment
- targeted training and personal development

- organising social events that promote diversity awareness and inclusion
- empowering black staff, learners and communities to influence decisions that affect them.

                              (The Commission for Black Staff in Further
                                                     Education 2002)

Training interviewers

It is important that all those involved in recruitment and selection of staff have undergone equality training. Those targeted should include governors, middle and senior management, local authority representatives and human resources personnel.

It might seem that, having such a long list of professionals in the selection and recruitment of staff, equality training might not be necessary, but it is. In my 16-year experience as a staff interviewer for a secondary school I have met many interviewers who had not the slightest idea about the meaning of equality, never mind how this should be put into practice. However, they cannot be blamed for not knowing, as they were not trained. After complaints, the school decided to make it obligatory for all interviewers to have training. Courses were set up for those interviewers who had no training and those that had went on yearly refresher sessions.

Selection and recruitment panels should be representative of the college's diversity. Panels should include members from BME groups, different sexes, disabled members and staff unions.

What equal opportunities recruitment training should include

- Introduction to the college's race equality policy, including how the college is promoting race equality, a discussion of the RRAA 2000 and the college's duty to the act.
- Introductions to structural racism in British society and why the RRAA 2000 was necessary.
- Information regarding why it is important to tackle under-representation of BME staff.
- Explanations of the legal requirements and the implications for short-listing and interviewing.

- Identification and explanation about which questions should be used when interviewing.
- Explanations of stereotypes and challenges to these should be made clear so that interviewers understand that assumptions should not be made during the interview or anywhere else in the college.

Good practice for recruitment and selection

- Line managers should decide whether posts fall within positive action targets and implement strategies for this.
- Managers should draw up job descriptions which give a clear and concise description of the job.
- Managers should list all the duties and responsibilities of each position.
- Job descriptions should have nothing which is directly or indirectly discriminatory.
- Job descriptions should be examined and, where necessary, adjusted to meet the needs of targeted groups.
- Care must be taken to cover only essential requirements and to separate 'essential' from desirable.
- Attention must be paid to unnecessary bars for targeted groups, for example specific length of UK residence should not be a requirement.
- There should be no differentiation between UK qualifications and the equivalent abroad, provided that they are recognized by the DfES.
- Age restrictions must not be mentioned in advertisements and should not be a job requirement.
- Adverts should have positive action statements and be published in national daily as well as BME media, such as *Eastern Eye, The Voice* and *New Nation*.
- All permanent posts must be advertised externally – an exception would be if redeployment is necessary.
- All applicants should be sent an equal opportunities monitoring form with the college application form.
- On receipt of the completed application the equal opportunity form should be detached by a member of personnel not involved in the recruitment process.

- Short lists should be selected in accordance with equal opportunity principles. Decisions should be recorded on short-listing assessment forms and returned to human resources for retention and monitoring.
- Those short-listing and interviewing should have had training in equal opportunities and appointment procedures.
- At the interview questions asked should relate only to the person's qualifications and to the job description.
- Panel members should not ask questions on candidate's marriage prospects, religion, sexual orientation, care arrangements for children, political views or family plans.
- BME applicants should not be asked questions which directly or indirectly discriminate, such as those about UK customs and cultural practices, unless these are important for the job.
- Candidates should be assessed against the requirements of the job, irrespective of their age, race, ethnic origin, religion, sex, marital status, family commitments, sexual orientation or disability.
- All documents relating to job applications should be kept by the college for at least six months.

How to carry out good practice interviews

All recruitment and selection procedures should follow the college's race equality criteria. There are a number of selection tools used in recruitment, which include:

- interviews
- presentation
- discussion interviews on specific topics
- group discussion
- references
- assessment.

Interviews
When using interviews, in addition to general good practice the following points are important:

- Different roles for members of the interview panel should be agreed, e.g. who will chair the interview, who will open and close it and what questions each of the panel will ask.
- The selection panel should agree and familiarize themselves with the core set of interview questions and each candidate's application form in advance. The same core set of questions should be posed to every candidate. However, additional questioning and probing are likely to be needed. This should focus on enabling the candidate to provide evidence to support the selection criteria that may not, for example, have been prominent in their application form or at previous interviews/discussions.
- Agree how notes will be recorded during the interview.
- Individual members of the interview panel should be allowed time immediately following the interview to review their own notes and experience and rate the candidate against the selection criteria without conferring. Only once this has been completed should the interview panel jointly discuss their ratings. This approach helps to minimize bias and subjectivity in the decision-making process.
- Ensure that no aspect of the interview unfairly discriminates against any individual candidate, in terms of the interview, location, timing, room set-up and questions.
- Candidates may be asked to make a presentation to the selection panel and/or to a wider audience, including members of staff and students. Care should be taken to consider how the feedback from the audience will be gathered and used in the decision-making process:
  - The audience may be asked to rate the candidate against a small number of specific criteria, such as communication and presentation skills and the ability to inspire confidence.
  - Records of feedback/rating and what weight this carried in influencing the selection panels decision on each candidate should be kept.
- The selection panel may wish to discuss particular issues in more depth with candidates in order to test, for example, the ability to support the values and strategy of the institution.

Record-keeping and monitoring

A record should be kept for every appointment. This should detail how selection and non-selection decisions have been made, including the criteria and evidence on which they were based. This provides evidence, should a complaint or appeal be brought against the recruitment and selection process. It will also ensure that colleges are prepared to comply with the Data Protection Act 1998 and the Freedom of Information Act 2000.

In accordance with these Acts, job applicants may be entitled to access interview notes on written request. The record should include, at least, a summary of the evidence used against the selection criteria as a basis for making acceptance and non-selection decisions on every candidate at each stage of the selection process. It is recommended that records be kept for the length of time in which ligation may be brought, namely six years.

A college monitoring results

A college began monitoring as part of its commitment to equal opportunities. Its data collection included information regarding racial group, gender, disability, nationality, residential status (international/home) and grade. Detailed analysis of this data demonstrated that staff from black and ethnic minorities, particularly men, were underrepresented in full-time and permanent teaching posts and within senior management.

The college decided to investigate the problems in more detail and found that:

- more than half of BME staff were employed in part-time or hourly-paid posts
- BME staff made three times as many applications for full-time posts, but very few reached the interview stage
- monitoring showed that those appointed to full-time jobs were usually young, white and had a conventional education
- despite having been more highly qualified than white colleagues, BME staff were concentrated in certain subject areas, such as those relating to continued educational

studies, such as teaching basic skills and English as a second language
- BME staff took twice as long as white colleagues to gain promotion
- they had fewer opportunities to gain career development and training.

Examples of positive action

A college, having conducted ethnic monitoring and assessment, found that BME staff were disadvantaged because of college policies and practices. As a result the college:
- employed a senior manager to be in charge of race equality
- reviewed and revised existing policies and procedures relating to recruitment and selection
- implemented formal selection procedures, with advertisements for jobs both internally and externally
- made sure that those involved in the selection process had equal opportunity training
- opened up career development training to all part-time and hourly-paid staff by paying for the hours spent travelling and for attendance
- reviewed and revised its policy and procedure regarding the creation of teaching posts and for deciding whether they were full or part-time positions
- spoke to all part-time BME staff and encouraged them to apply for full-time posts that became available
- set up an equal opportunity group, which included BME staff and union representatives, who would report to the senior manager and coordinator
- introduced a mentoring scheme for BME staff and other groups who required them
- made sure that a monitoring report was produced and published once a year. The findings were used to set employment targets and training courses
- drew up a positive action plan which offers BME staff management training.

A college strategy for improving representation and retention

We are now monitoring more closely the ethnic profile of staff across the college and also our recruitment. This has shown a year-on-year increase in the number of staff from non-white backgrounds, although we need to increase the numbers of black applicants to the college. We are reviewing all our staffing policies and procedures to ensure that they are non-discriminatory. In particular, we have reviewed the staff recruitment policy and completely revised our staff application form to ensure that all personal details are on a separate, tear-off slip. We are starting to monitor staff retention more closely and the turnover of staff by department and ethnicity.

We have invited staff to join a support network to help them raise any issues of concern in a safe environment. Our staff development policy is well-established and last year the college invested money in training. We encourage all staff to apply for jobs that are advertised internally and externally. We are running a course on how staff can best apply for jobs, which looks at how to complete application forms and present themselves at interview.

We have a very thorough system of staff review rather than appraisal, where the focus is on personal development. All new staff have mentors appointed to help them through the induction period. This is being rolled out to support staff. The college has a well-established grievance policy, which has been used. The college sets targets in relation to equality. This is ambitious and we know that it will take a very long time to get the staffing profile in line with that of our students.

(HR manager, Avaley 1994)

Summary

In this chapter we examined the issues of recruitment and retention of BME staff. Looking at the Commission for Black Staff in FE report (2002), we realize that colleges need to have a clear anti-racist policy on this issue. Despite the passing of the RRAA 2000 colleges are slow in promoting race equality.

This chapter argues that monitoring and assessment of all staff by racial group in areas of recruitment, retention, promotion and careers development should be carried out. This should be followed by the setting of race equality employment targets. We have given advice on how this should be done.

6 Career development training

Black managers in FE

No one is prevented from promotion in this college if they have the necessary qualifications and experience. Career development training is available to everyone who wants it, including black and minority ethnic staff. I, as a middle manager, was encouraged by a white senior colleague to apply for senior management, but I refused. I preferred to keep teaching and did not want to become a paper pusher. The college has two senior black managers, one in IT, and there are two other prospective black senior managers waiting in the wings until there is a vacancy.

(FE black manager)

Senior black managers

The above quote is an example of the good practice found in some colleges. But underrepresentation of black staff within managerial positions is still a problem in FE, despite the RRAA 2000. Lee Jasper, Director of Equalities of the Greater London Authority, argued that, at the current rate of progress, equality in public service organizations in London would be achieved *between 2045 and 2095*. He said he was not willing to wait that long. Jasper argues that the issue is not how good the race policy is, but whether the policy is being promoted and *what progress has been made* (*Leadership and Diversity – Changing Organisational Cultures*, Conference Report, 18 May 2004: 8).

Unequal promotion

The underrepresentation of BME managers in FE is a result of institutional racism within colleges. Some college managers and senior staff have a stereotyped image of black staff, as one line manager observed:

the college is good at managing diversity at the lower end, with black and disabled lecturers. It is as if they see that they can employ disabled and black people at the lower end, but actually there is nothing stopping diverse people from being senior managers, but they don't see that.

(FE manager LSRC 2005)

How to improve the number of BME senior managers in FE

To improve the number of BME senior managers in FE:

- managers and senior staff should be fully committed to promoting race equality. Colleges will have to embrace positive action programmes
- colleges should challenge stereotypes
- colleges should ensure that all staff recruitment is carried out in accordance with the college's race equality policy
- colleges should make sure that all BME staff including part-time workers are given the opportunity for promotion and career development

FE is 'not alone'

Sir Andrew Foster, in his review of Further Education (2005), summed up the situation: 'There are so few Black and Minority Ethnic staff at middle management level that it will take a very long time for more staff from underrepresented groups to reach senior positions without a fast track programme that has credibility.'

Foster also observed that the underrepresentation of BME groups in senior management is not the preserve of colleges alone, because 'just as startling is the complete absence of any Minority Ethnic presence on the senior management teams of all the key national organisations in the system, including the DfES, LSC, AOC, Ofsted, CEL, ALI, ALP, LSDA and ACM and only a small number on the boards of these organisations' (Foster 2005: 22).

What's worrying about this situation is that these organization are not immune to institutional racism and, like colleges, do not seem to be in a hurry to change. If organizations such as the DfES and the LSC have no senior managers from BME groups, how can they expect colleges and higher educational institutions to do so?

Positive action programmes

Positive action programmes have been misunderstood over the years as positive discrimination, as explained in previous chapters. In a recent report by the LSC, March 2005, many colleges refused to set race equality targets, because they believed them to be positive discrimination, an unlawful practice.

What is positive action?

Positive action allows organizations to provide training and encouragement for people of a particular racial group that has been underrepresented in certain occupations or grades over the previous year. Monitoring, secondment and work shadowing are all positive action programmes which are used and can be used within FE colleges to improve the number of BME staff in senior management positions.

Positive action can also be used for women, the disabled and any group that is underrepresented in certain jobs.

Mentoring, work shadowing and secondment should be part of career development and be offered to all staff, including BME groups. However, in areas such as senior management where black people are grossly underrepresented managers are required to target this group for training as part of the college's positive equal opportunity action plan.

Providing opportunity

Having the opportunity to undergo mentoring, work shadowing and secondment will help BME staff who want to move forward in their career. It will give them the opportunity to gain confidence, skills and the experience to apply for and get senior jobs in the FE sector.

With the support of managers and senior staff, positive action programmes should become an integral part of staff development. This will increase diversity within colleges' senior management and staff.

How to prepare staff

Positive action programmes can be contentious, so equal opportunity managers should prepare all staff for this. Managers should have ensured that:

- all staff have had race equality training and at least half a day's introductory course, which should explain the legal duties of the RRAA 2000
- the college's Race Equality Policy has been introduced and explained
- positive action programmes and what they involve has been discussed, informing all staff about the reasons why such programmes are necessary. This will raise awareness and inform staff about the college's responsibility and their own towards race equality. With raised awareness, managers will find it easier to target BME staff for positive action and white staff will not see these programmes as positive discrimination.

Disabled staff

The preparation of staff before positive action programmes should include information on other disadvantaged groups, like the disabled who, like BME groups, are underrepresented in management and other senior posts in FE. The disabled should be involved in positive action programmes which will give them the skills to compete for senior posts. Training should be given to all staff to raise awareness of the Disability Act 1995 and the legal requirements of the college.

Practising equality

Without proper staff induction, these programmes may cause friction between the majority and minority groups, while what they should be doing is to create an equal and fair environment for all staff. Managers should stress the potential benefits of these programmes and that targeted action does not mean that some staff have been unfairly excluded. It should also be stressed that the reasons why BME staff have been targeted is because in the past they have been unfairly treated due to college policies.

Black staff reassurance

Black staff will also have to be reassured that they are not singled out because they are 'failures'. Managers will have to communicate the issues of past discrimination and that it is the college's policy to redress the balance. Managers should not forget to explain the demands of the RRAA 2000 on the college.

Black staff will understand the need for race equality, because most have been victims of racist practice, witting or unwitting. They will want reassurance about their entitlement to career development and that positive action programmes, such as mentoring and work shadowing, are important to help them compete for senior posts.

Positive action programmes: Who should be involved?
- Managers should communicate with staff unions about the proposed programme.
- The college's equal opportunity group, if there is one, should be informed.
- Black staff focus groups should be involved. Such groups are usually well informed about equality issues and know the difference between positive discrimination and positive action. They can help managers to inform staff about the issues and the proposed positive action programme.
- Communication between the manager in charge of race equality and line managers is very important, before any positive action programmes begin. There should be discussion about the programme, why it is being implemented, when it is being implemented and how many participants are expected.

Finance

Issues on cover and finance will also have to be discussed, as colleges will have to provide both for participants in positive action programmes, including part-timers. If finance is a problem, colleges should be able to approach the LSC, but more importantly it would be useful in future for funds to be put aside for positive action programmes. In order to stop complaints that BME staff are getting preferential treatment, it may be wise also to have similar courses for other underrepresented groups, such as disabled staff, so that they are seen to be benefiting from positive actions programmes as well.

Black staff career development

The Commission for Black Staff in Further Education report (2002) highlighted the underrepresentation of black staff in colleges, especially in senior management. As a result, organizations like the Black Leadership Initiative (BLI) and concerned colleges began to address the problem. They did so by setting up or getting involved with professional development initiatives, including mentoring, secondment, work shadowing and professional development workshops.

Professional development

The BLI was the leader in the professional development of black staff in FE between 2002 and 2004. The BLI was funded by the LSC. The intention of the programme was to address

the underrepresentation of Black staff at managerial level, by developing and implementing a strategic approach to support the recruitment, retention and development of Black staff into further leadership roles.

(reference document, *Shadowing Programme*, Black Leadership Initiative–Background Information, 2004)

What is mentoring?

Mentoring has emerged as a vehicle for translating learning into action. Mentoring not only provides a conduit for action, but a way to think about acting; rather than take on the overwhelming weight of social issues, mentors are afforded the opportunity to connect with a single individual (Freedman 1999).

Mentoring as a form of career development is one of the best forms of help and support which can be given to BME staff in FE who want to move forward in their careers. Although some colleges were involved in the scheme through the BLI, what is needed is a well-organized nationwide mentoring schemes within FE colleges.

The limitations

Mentoring has become more than just advisory and counselling programmes for employees and students; it has become big business and has expanded enormously over the last 30 years in North America and the United Kingdom. It has become an important part of education and training, professional development, business, management, teaching, healthcare and helping disadvantaged young people in cities (Colley 2003: 1)

Colley stated that mentoring has 'acquired a mythical status, suggesting almost superhuman powers, to transform the mentee in the face of all odds'. The mentoring movement has grown into a social movement, seen by some as a cheap and easy route, a *quick fix* to long-standing social problems (Freedman 1999).

There is a limitation in terms of what mentoring can do for urban disadvantaged young people and even BME teachers in FE, who are undervalued because of discriminatory practices in colleges. Long-standing problems such as racial and class discrimination, which result in inequality in society, have to change and no amount of mentoring will be able to right these wrongs.

The advantages

However, a mentoring programme used by colleges in further education as career development and positive action programmes for BME groups has a lot of advantages, which cannot be dismissed, and neither can mentoring in general. As Freedman puts it:

mentoring constitutes a window of hope, a glimpse, not only of our better selves but of a potentially better society, one built not only on individual acts of kindness but on a broader set of programmes, policies and institutions.

(Freedman 1999: 11)

Mentors

'A mentor is an experienced and trusted adviser, one who trains and counsels new employees or students. The name originates from Mentor, the adviser of the young Telemachus, in Homer's *Odyssey*' (*Concise Oxford English Dictionary*).

Good mentoring schemes make sure that those who put themselves forward for mentoring are suitable and receive proper training. The role of the mentor is a skilled one. The job of the mentor is to guide and support the mentee towards achieving their goals. Mentors will need support and training before taking on a mentee. They will have to learn the practical skills and knowledge needed to help their mentee.

Mentors need:

- to have good listening skills and be able to question and answer questions honestly and sensitively, without being patronizing
- to be able to effectively manage and review their work with mentees
- to help mentees to clarify their goals and career plans and put these into practice.

Mentoring training

- Mentoring training and workshops should be led by experienced trainers.
- There should be a balance of activities between theory and practice and enough time given for all participants to get involved in group discussion.
- Role play is a very important tool for mentoring training. Although not liked by some, it gives participants some experience of what it is like to be in someone else's shoes.
- Training courses should help mentors to feel confident about their role as mentors.
- Programmes should offer education and information on race/equality and positive action.

The object of training is to ensure that participants understand:

- the legal requirements of the RRAA 2000
- structural racism in society
- institutional racism in the education system and how it affects progress of black staff into senior management
- how mentoring, as part of a positive action programme, can redress the balance
- the relationship needed between mentor and mentee in order to be successful.

Mentoring black staff

Mentoring BME staff for senior management posts in colleges needs special skills and understanding on the part of the mentor. The BLI, in its mentoring programme, matches individuals with senior managers, including principals from outside institutions, to act as mentors. They offer tailored 'one to one support to mentees to identify development goals' and how to achieve them (LSC 2004).

Time requirement

Mentoring programmes usually have a minimum requirement for mentors and mentees to meet, ranging from once a week to once a month. In the case of the BLI scheme, the numbers of contact hours between mentors and mentees were ten hours minimum and fifteen hours maximum, either face to face or over the phone. Mentor and mentee meet 'at least once a month for formal contact' and informal contact, as suitable for both parties. Mentoring lasts between six and twelve months (Black Leadership Initiative Pilot, October 2002–August 2004).

Other mentoring schemes, such as the National Mentoring Consortium (NMC), whose programme mentors BME students, have a duration of only six months, but formal contact is more frequent, with one to two hours per week (www.heacademy.ac.uk/2612htm, 12 July 2005).

Matching mentors and mentees

The process of matching mentor to mentee is a very important one. Getting this wrong can lead to the mentor becoming more of a disadvantage than advantage. The skills of the mentor should be matched to the requirements of the mentee.

A shortlist of mentors should be provided, from which mentees can pick the one who will be most useful to them. Once paired, mentor and mentee should meet before they begin to work more closely together. For such relationships to work, they must be compatible.

Most mentees in FE who completed mentoring programmes found it a useful exercise. They gained insight into their chosen career and learnt about planning, progression, goal setting, CV writing, networking and interview techniques.

White mentors, black mentees

Most mentoring schemes have more white than black mentors. The reason is quite simple, as there are more white staff in managerial and senior positions in every sector of western society. Therefore it makes good business sense for mentoring schemes to take on those who have the most skills and experience that mentees are looking for.

Cultural differences

The questions that need to be addressed are:

- Can white mentors overcome the cultural differences, including black people's experiences of structural and institutional racism, in order to help?
- Although race training is given to all mentors, is enough time given to raise the awareness of white mentors about the disadvantages BME groups face daily in colleges and the wider community?
- Will race training leave white mentors feeling guilty, angry or as though they are under attack?
- Should the facts be watered down so as not to make people feel uncomfortable?
- Will race training be of any benefit if the facts are distorted?
- How can race training on mentoring courses be sensitive and positive? To do so, courses will need to give the facts without blaming individuals. Promoting equality should be a collective responsibility with each person doing what they can to change the system which discriminates.

Positive contribution

White members who have put themselves forward to help black staff career development are making a positive contribution to the promotion of racial equality. The outcome of white staff mentoring black mentees depends to some extent upon whether anti-racist training has raised the white mentors' awareness of the black experiences within colleges and society in general. In cases where this has not been achieved, it might be that such courses require more time to put across the message than most mentoring schemes can afford.

Some mentoring schemes do, however, manage to get across the message of how institutional racism affects BME staff. One white mentor said, after a race awareness course, 'It opened my eyes to what my colleagues from Ethnic Minorities face every day' (LSC 2004: 38).

Black mentors, black mentees

Black mentors are very special in any mentoring scheme concerned with the career progression of black staff in education, because:

- those that are chosen to be mentors are usually well-qualified. They have had to work twice as hard to get qualifications and promotions
- like mentees, they have had experiences of racism within not only educational institutions, but society
- they have managed to overcome these barriers and have made it; as such they are role models for black mentees, whether they like it or not
- black mentors can empathize with BME mentees and their experiences.

However, there are other forms of discrimination which have the same effect as racism in denying equality. For example, prejudice against disabled people, ageism, homophobia and sexual discrimination. White mentors who have had personal experiences of any of these are sometimes able to relate to the black experience – but not always.

The issue of racism

It seems that in most cases black mentees were more able to raise the issues of *racism and discrimination* with their black mentors. One black mentee said:

You don't have to have a Black mentor all the time, but it was important in our relationship. My mentor's own experiences of race and racism were important in helping me to understand my situation.

(LSC 2004: 36)

Work shadowing

Work shadowing and mentoring often go together. A mentor allows their mentee to shadow them doing their job, thus giving the mentee added practical support, insight and experience into how the job is done. This is usually a position or career path which the mentee is aspiring to undertake and therefore is an invaluable experience to have.

Some participants undertake shadowing schemes because they want to get experience and knowledge of a certain career in which BME staff are underrepresented, such as senior managerial positions, or employment as an Ofsted inspector.

Criteria

The criteria needed for selection on a shadowing programme include:

- having the willingness to take responsibility for your own learning
- actively seeking promotion and career development and readiness to move into leadership
- the ability to express yourself verbally and in writing
- being in a position in your career where shadowing will be beneficial and is likely to result in promotion
- willingness to receive feedback and advice
- the employing college principal has to provide a reference demonstrating that the prospective participant will be able to benefit from the programme
- the employing college will have to be willing to release the shadow for between five to ten days to take part in the programme
- the participant will have to be a permanent member of the college, either in a full or part-time position.

The BLI Shadowing Programme 2002–04 took between five to ten days and participants were placed within one of the learning and skills sector agencies such as Ofsted, ALI and the LSC. The project matched participants in an area where they would get the best opportunity and 'practical benefits', in terms of their career development.

Shadows who did not get a mentor were offered one after the programme, who could provide 'one to one guidance and coaching support', to further participants towards their goals (Black Leadership Initiative Shadowing Programme, 2002–4: 2).

Secondment

Like mentoring and work shadowing, secondment is part of a positive action programme which helps underrepresented groups in certain jobs gain the experiences needed to apply for and get jobs in these areas:

- Programmes are carried out in colleges, universities, businesses and schools.
- In FE colleges secondment programmes are being carried out, in part, to meet the demands of the RRAA 2000.
- These programmes can be run within colleges or organized by outside organizations such as the BLI.
- Secondees can be placed in middle and senior management posts for periods ranging from one term to one year.
- The aim is to match the secondees with projects that will provide them with practical experiences that will help further their careers.
- As in work shadowing, the participant secondee is responsible for identifying their own career development needs and, with the guidance and support of their line managers and mentor, work towards achieving these goals.
- Secondees, like work shadowing participants, gain practical experiences by being in the scheme.
- They can gain managerial experience and are able to see the workings of senior management.
- These experiences will give participants some knowledge regarding the work of senior managers and the skills they, as potential managers and leaders, will need.

The most important aspect of mentoring, work shadowing and secondment is whether these courses meet the objectives of helping black staff gain skills and experiences to help them move into senior management. The evaluation of the BLI 2004 programme found that the skills and knowledge participants gained helped participants obtain jobs which were 'previously perceived as being out of reach' (LSC 2004: 45).

Providing placements
If positive programmes are to work, college managers must be in full support, leading from the front and influencing other staff to favour such programmes.

The evaluation of the Black Leadership Initiative 2004 provides an insight into various responses of colleges who provided placements for these schemes. Most colleges that were questioned during the evaluation provided placements because they were committed to diversity and to helping 'Black and Minority Ethnic staff gain the skills they need, to move into every sector of further education'.

Negative view
- Some colleges providing placements took a negative view. One saw positive action programmes as being beneficial only to 'black staff' and not to 'the college'.
- They were unable to see that black staff and the college both gained from the programme.
- Some participants of these programmes reported that their 'line managers were not very supportive' and showed very little interest in the 'positive action programmes'.
- Some colleges were concerned that participants returning from positive action courses might find that 'progression routes might not be available, which might lead to frustration at not being able to use their experience' (LSC 2004: 10–12).
- There is also the possibility that those returning might be seen as race experts 'rather than a leader who has something to contribute to the college' (LSC 2004: 40).
- There is the old problem with positive action programmes designed for BME groups. They are generally not given much credibility, because they are seen as dealing only with black issues (Ainley 1994).

Opposing positive action

Managers of colleges, like editors, are probably not aware that structural racism is the reason why positive action programmes are necessary. The media, like educational institutions, employ very few black people, especially in senior positions: and positive action training is the one way to redress the balance.

Managers who oppose these programmes, whether in the media or educational institutions, are wittingly or unwittingly continuing the process of racism and are therefore part of the problem. In the case of educational institutions, managers who oppose such programmes are breaking the law.

Black managers

We could be forgiven for thinking that all would be well for BME staff that have made it up to management. We might think that the process from then onwards would be smooth and without discrimination. After all, most BME managers have had to work twice as long and hard as other colleagues to get into management, However, discrimination does not end when black staff become managers.

Favouritism

Those who are helped into management through positive action schemes, such as mentoring, work shadowing or secondment, sometimes find that colleagues think they have been promoted because they are black, as a result of favouritism through positive action programmes.

- College managers should have made sure all staff had training before the college took part in positive actions programmes, as I have argued earlier in this chapter.
- Managers should reiterate the colleges' responsibility to the RRAA 2000 and that doing these courses does not automatically lead to promotion.
- It should be explained that participants were only prepared and given the necessary advice and skills with which to compete with other applicants for senior positions.

Black managers facing resistance

Many black managers face resistance from all sectors of the college, including other managers, students, teaching and non-teaching staff. One black manager found that her colleagues changed when she was promoted:

It's as if they didn't expect a Black woman to be a manager. Some colleagues who used to speak to me began to ignore me in the staff room and the canteen. At first I couldn't understand why and suddenly I realised what was going on.

(Ainley 1994)

Others said that they are not allowed to make mistakes, unlike white managers. They are 'picked upon for the slightest error'. Senior managers and staff expect perfection. Jackie, a black manager in a London college told me: 'We have to be twice as good and work twice as hard as white managers. We feel we can't make a mistake, we can't be human, we have to be superhuman' (Ainley 1994).

The Commission for Black Staff in FE heard evidence from black staff that some colleges had negative views about their competence without any justification. This led to 'overcritical and over-controlling management styles'. Black staff reported that they were constantly under pressure to 'prove themselves' (2002: 56).

How to deal with resistance

- Senior managers should be aware of the resistance BME staff, especially those in management, may face from other staff and students.
- First, they should make sure they are not part of the problem by putting pressure on black staff.
- Support should be given to all staff facing harassment or resistance.
- Staff should have information about the institution's bullying and harassment procedures and how to complain.
- All new staff, including managers, should be given the name of a contact who will give help, information and advice if needed. They should also be given a staff handbook, providing details of college policies, including those on race

equality, anti–bullying, harassment, behaviour codes, managers' responsibilities, entitlements and procedures.

- Information relating to staff meetings, training and college events should be supplied.
- Senior or line managers must ensure that all staff, including new managers, get effective induction and support, even if they are not new to the college and have worked in another capacity.
- Staff should be informed about the new manager's position, responsibilities and role in relation to other staff.
- Senior managers must be aware that all staff, regardless of age, race, gender, disability and religion, are entitled to work within a safe and supportive environment.
- BME managers should be supported against discrimination, be it unwitting or not.
- Educating all college staff is one way of reducing possible discrimination
- College managers should encourage BME staff who feel isolated to join groups such as the network for black managers, the college equal opportunity or other focus groups.

Case study 1

Mentor

John, a senior manager of a London college, offered to be a mentor on a positive action programme. He was aware of the underrepresentation of BME staff in senior managerial jobs and wanted to help.

Being white, John was a little nervous at first that he might be seen as inexperienced regarding the issues which affect black staff. He admitted his fears to those administering the programme, but found that all mentors were offered training which included cultural diversity, the legal requirements of the RRAA 2000, and institutional and structural racism. He found the training to be open, relaxed and honest. The subjects were tackled sensitively, which made him more confident and better able to understand the problems black staff experienced and why.

John found the mentoring experience rewarding and a pleasure, because he was able to listen and help another human being and made a difference. He said he enjoyed meeting and supporting his mentee, with whom he had a good relationship. He had learnt a lot from his mentee and gained a lot of skills by being a mentor.

He was rewarded for his efforts when shortly after the programme ended John's mentee applied for and got a job in senior management.

Case study 2

Mentee

Margaret, a black mentee on a positive action programme, had been trying for years to move into management. She had been a full-time lecturer in continuing education for five years and had worked at the college for two years previously as a part-time member of staff.

When she was promoted to full-time, she had hoped to continue her career progression into management. She asked her line manager several times to go on career development courses, but was turned down. The reason given was that there were others more senior than herself who had to go, or that the college did not have the funds to cover her absence. Margaret began to think of leaving.

The mentoring programme came just in time and she was allowed to join it because it was directed at BME staff.

Margaret attended a two-day induction course for mentees and was told that there were black and white mentors. She did not mind what colour her mentor was: all that mattered was if the person could help her move forward.

In the end, she was matched with a black mentor, but she did not bring up the issue of racism. It was the mentor who did, by telling her about her own experiences, to which

> Margaret related. Margaret said her mentor supported her by helping her to look at and challenge barriers in a positive way and showing her how to progress in her career.

Summary

Here we looked at career development training for BME staff in FE colleges, who are underrepresented in management and senior positions. We examined positive action courses and found that, although they have been largely successful for BME staff, some colleges had a negative view of them. These institutions held the view that positive action programmes helped the individual, but not the college.

The chapter looked at the problem of mentoring and whether white mentors are able to overcome individual and institutional racism in order to help black staff in their career development. We also examined the role of black managers in FE and their experience of racism.

7 Promoting race/equality

Managing diversity

Managing diversity has been problematic for decades, not only in colleges and HE institutions, but in the media and multinational corporations. In general, many colleges have resisted change, despite the passing of the RRAA 2000. Some writers have argued that legislation which demands equality and diversity is politically naive because, instead of bringing about change, it risks provoking the opposite effect (Dass and Parker 1999).

Diversity report

The Learning and Skills Research Centre (LSRC) report 2005 showed that many FE managers and leaders have not fully grasped the importance and the positive effect of diversity. There is a gap between those managers who agree with diversity and those who neither do nor can understand the other point of view.

Comments against diversity include:

1. Diversity is not relevant, because we don't have a high percentage of ethnic minority staff or students.
2. Diversity is not relevant, because people should be appointed to management roles on merit.
3. Promoting diversity will have a negative impact on the performance of the college.
4. While diversity should be encouraged, it should not be over-encouraged.

Why is diversity important?

1. In a multicultural multiracial society diversity is fundamental to all leadership.

2. A diverse staff can better meet the needs of a diverse student population.
3. A college which has a diversity of students and staff will create a better understanding between people of different races and culture.

Litigation
Many FE college managers are more concerned about the fear of litigation than with taking any action to promote race/equality. Any dealings they have with equality are merely coincidental. Diversity is seen only through the needs of students. They are unable to see, or do not want to, that the employment of a more diverse workforce will also help learners and makes good business sense. Their interest in student diversity is not because they believe in equality; it is purely financial and short-term.

Policy changes
Policy changes are used as an excuse by some managers not to promote race/equality issues. They complain that the workload and pressures to meet financial and achievement targets means that they have not got the time for diversity issues. They have instead to concentrate on activities which will lead to funding and in some cases survival (LSRC 2005: 102–3).

We cannot deny that the pressures for funding and achievement can be all-consuming for managers and teachers in FE, but race/equality issues were never high on most colleges' agenda even when there were not such demands.

A moral case for diversity
While a number of FE managers and leaders understand the need for fairness and equality, too many are not able to see, or do not want to see, diversity as a moral issue. UCU argued that colleges have suffered from 'transactional leadership or macho management' (LSRC 2005: 106–7) and that this is what lies at the heart of the problem.

Class issues
Why is it so difficult for leaders and management in FE and HE institutions to embrace race/equality? Maybe we have to look more closely at those who is running the show.

They are mostly white, male, middle-class, Christian, heterosexual and able-bodied. As it stands, they represent a very narrow view of the world. It could be argued that their backgrounds have buried their humanity and the moral need for equality towards those who do not share their skin colour or background. Managers and leaders of FE should be persuaded by all means necessary that diversity is good. The reality is that there isn't an option to do nothing, because it is neither 'tenable or ethical on educational or business grounds' (LSRC 2005: 100–1).

Action to be taken

1. As described in Chapters 3 and 5, managers should take the monitoring of staff and students seriously, and it should be followed by assessment.
2. Educational bodies such as the DfES and the LSC should take the responsibility to see that management and leadership of FE carry out these duties. Colleges should be given help and a reasonable time limit.
3. The sector needs a definition of diversity that all organizations funded by the LSC can follow.
4. Colleges should be judged by the action taken to promote organizational diversity and equality among staff and students.
5. As explained in Chapter 2, race and diversity training is important for all staff, including managers. The Centre for Excellence in Leadership should provide training and advice for all managers on the requirements of:
   - the RRAA 2000
   - the Discrimination Act 1975
   - the Human Rights Act 1998
   - the Special Needs and Disability Act (SENDA) 2001, which also amends the Disability Discrimination Act (DDA) 1995)
   - the European Employment Directive, which requires member states to outlaw discrimination in employment on the grounds of sexual orientation and religion or belief from December 2003, and on the grounds of age by December 2006.
6. As mentioned in Chapter 6, positive action programmes

such as mentoring and work shadowing should be used to help in the career development of staff from disadvantaged groups.

Governors

Recent reports, (Foster 2006 and BTEG 2005) suggest that governors, like FE managers, are just as reluctant to promote race equality. Some see positive action programmes as positive discrimination. Like managers, governors also need race and diversity training, if they are to persuade managers to abide by the law. Governors have to become aware of their responsibility to the college. They are responsible for ensuring that:

1. members of the corporation reflect the diversity of the community the college serves
2. the college's strategic plan includes a commitment to race equality
3. they are aware of the corporation's statutory responsibilities in relation to race/equality legislation as an employer and service provider
4. they receive and respond to the racial group monitoring information on learners and staff.
5. the principal and senior staff set race/equality employment targets measured against appropriate benchmarks.

How to make college corporations more diverse
1. Colleges should go into the community and actively seek members from underrepresented groups.
2. They should inform the community of vacancies and tell them that they are welcome to apply.
3. Information can be posted in churchs, mosques, synagogues, town halls, local newspapers, mother and baby groups, women's groups and disabled organizations.
4. The colleges should support applications from single mothers/ parents by giving financial assistance for childcare and travel.
5. Meetings should be held at varied times and not only late evenings, when some women, because of religious requirements, are not able to be out of the home.

6. Travelling expenses should be given to all governors who need it. There should also be facilities for disabled people, who should be encouraged to become governors.

Race and HE

Pretending it isn't happening

Like FE colleges, HE institutions have a duty under the RRAA 2000 to 'eliminate unlawful racial discrimination and to promote equality of opportunity and good relations between persons of different racial groups' (CRE 2004: 45).

We have established in this book that the success of the RRAA 2000 in FE colleges is patchy, but is HE doing any better? John Grace, in his article 'We remain almost invisible', reported that universities, even after the RRAA, were 'still turning a blind eye to racism, as if it could not possibly exist among the liberal intellectual elite' (*Guardian*, 14 February 2004).

Turning a blind eye to racism may be one reason why HE is not willing to carry out a study on itself into race equality as FE has done.

BME students in HE

Most universities, old or new, are trying to attract overseas students, and many are BME. The reason is simple: overseas students bring in money. As a result of institutional racism and resistance to the promotion of race/equality, older universities in Britain have a low black student population, less than 10 per cent. They are most likely to accept white candidates and to a lesser extent Chinese candidates from a group of similarly qualified applicants. British Afro-Caribbeans, Asians and African students are more likely to be studying at one of the new universities – 21 per cent (CRE 2004).

On the other hand, FE colleges do go out of their way to attract students from local communities, because one of their duties is to provide skills and training for employment. Figures show that the numbers of BME students rose in further education colleges by 12 per cent in 1998 to 14 per cent in 1999. The largest figure is in London at 36 per cent, followed by 15.9 per cent in the West Midlands. In the inner cities the figures of BME students in some colleges can be as high as 80 per cent.

Promoting black staff in HE

Like black managers in further education, black academics who get promotion sometimes experience verbal abuse from white colleagues, who believe that they get the job because they are black. Cecil Wright, Professor of Sociology at Nottingham Trent University, explained that soon after she was given her professorship she received a call from a white colleague, who was incensed that she had been promoted. He told her that she 'had been promoted only because she was Black' (Chris Bunting, 'Distinct Lack of Ebony', *The Times Higher Educational Supplement*, 22 October 2004).

Professor Wright's response in the article to the issue of HE institutions and race is direct and uncompromising:

The situation in academia with regard to race is absolutely disgusting and shocking. In the Health service or in schools, it would not be allowed to happen because there is more scrutiny. Universities are able to hide away because they are seen as liberal institutions.

Recruitment and retention of BME staff in HE

There are similar problems in both further and higher education institutions in relation to the hiring, retention and promotion of BME staff. However, FE colleges employ fewer BME staff compared to HE institutions.

FE worse at recruiting black staff

The Commission for Black Staff in FE 2002 found that black staff constitute 6.9 per cent of the overall staff population in FE colleges as compared to the 10.9 per cent in HE (HE statistics 2005). When we consider that there are more FE colleges than universities, some with more than 30 per cent BME students, this is not a fact that FE can be proud of. However, HE institutions have been attacked frequently within the educational sections of newspapers for their inflexibility and slow response to racial inequality and the RRAA 2000.

FE and HE's slow response to race equality

Criticism of HE institutions and their slow response to race equality did not go unnoticed, and Luton University announced that 'almost one in five academics' at the 'University, are from Ethnic

Minority backgrounds, almost twice the proportion of academic sector averages' (T. Wainwright, *The Times Higher Educational Supplement*, 15 July 2005).

But the problem does not end here, because reports show that, even if BME staff get promoted, most are in the lower sectors of academia. They make up only 17 per cent of researchers, 9 per cent of lecturers, 6 per cent of senior lecturers, 4.4 per cent of professors, and are paid less than their white colleagues (*The Times Higher Educational Supplement*, 22 October 2004).

A study by the Association of University Teachers (AUT) in 2000 found that:

nearly a quarter of white lecturers earned more than £35,000 a year compared with 8 per cent of lecturers of African and Caribbean origin and over 12 per cent of lecturers of Asian origin. At the other end of the salary scale, 17 per cent of white lecturers earned £20,000 a year or less, while 20 per cent of African and Caribbean and 28 per cent of Asian lecturers were in this bracket.

In 2005 BME academics still earn less: 'On average they earn 88 per cent of their white colleagues' income.' A survey by the Equality Unit (2003) found that progress on race equality in higher education 'is sluggish with only 20 per cent making limited progress'.

There is discrimination against women too. They make up 40 per cent of academic staff, but earn on average of 86 per cent of what their male colleagues do (Education Guardian, *Guardian*, 22 November 2005).

Retention of BME staff

If universities pay BME academics less, do not like promoting them, give them greater workloads and undervalue their work, why should black academics want to stay? They do not, and many are leaving for the US.

They leave because of the lack of a multicultural curriculum and opportunities. Black academics who went to the United States found more research opportunities and better pay. They no longer have to 'struggle on a series of temporary contracts'.

Black academics leave because they are frustrated over the lack of black studies in British universities. They have long argued that black perspectives should be taught in schools, colleges and universities, but inequality still persist in the British educational system (M. Christian, *The Times Higher Educational Supplement*, 4 March 2005).

Shadowy discrimination in HE

Polly Curtis, in her article, 'Jobs for the white boys' (*Guardian*, 22 November 2005), explains that, in the competition for 'funding and to be published, the ivory towers of universities are rife with shadowy forms of discrimination', which promotes white male academics above their peers.

The Equality Unit, an organization that works with universities to promote best practice, is trying to persuade the sector to take race equality seriously by holding meetings and CRE-sponsored conferences. It might take more than meetings and conferences to make universities take race equality seriously, such as naming and shaming to make vice-chancellors take responsibility.

Race and trade unions

Thankfully, trade unions in the twenty-first century are taking equality and race issues seriously. Gone are the days when 'white trade unionists resisted employment of Black workers or insisted on a quota, generally 5 per cent'. Gone also are the days when there was an understanding between management and unions that the rule 'last in first out' should not apply to white workers when there were black immigrants employed (Fryer 1984: 37).

With unions as bedfellows of management, black workers in the 1950s and 1960s had no help from unions to fight discrimination and the racial attacks which were part of the popular racism of the day. Politicians like Enoch Powell inflamed and inspired racial hatred with his 'rivers of blood' speech at the time: 'Trade unionists, dockers and Smithfield porters downed tools and marched to the House of Commons in support of Powell's speech' (Fryer 1984: 384).

It was a shameful period in trade union history, but since then the unions have moved forward and now most trade unions, if not all, have a race equality policy, are promoting race equality in their own workforce and are supporting members in equality issues. This does not, however, mean that trade unions are perfect organizations, without fault or failings. It means that unions like UCU are doing all they can to give leadership in promoting race equality among their workforce and members.

The Commission's recommendations

The Commission for Black Staff in FE (2002) made eight recommendations to the trade unions in their full report, *Challenging Racism: Further Education Leading The Way* (p. 86).

The recommendations included:

- asking trade unions to provide *clear and decisive leadership*, by modelling best practice as employers
- setting race equality employment targets for trade unions, staff representatives and lay officers
- incorporating race equality into the formal negotiating arrangements they have with employers
- ensuring that paid officials and lay officers recognize the needs of their black members and actively support them against acts of institutional and individual racism.

The union response

In its response to the Commission's recommendations, UCU (2003) explained what they had done and were going to do over a number of years in providing clear leadership and commitment to race equality.

Recruitment

In the area of recruitment, UCU states that it has a very 'detailed recruitment and selection policy and that everyone on the selection panel has equal opportunity training. In order to get fair selection, personal details are detached from applications forms and all vacancies are advertised in the Black Press.'

The union carried out a staff equality audit in 2002, which showed that 10 out of 76 staff who returned the form were black. It stated that it will be carrying out staff equality audits every three years and, if black staff are underrepresented in any grades or locations, the union will set targets to rectify this.

In 2000 the union created an equality unit with full-time officers and administrators which is responsible for race equality issues. There is also a black staff group which is consulted on the issue of race.

Training and publishing

UCU organizes race equality training for paid officers and branch representatives. It also trains representatives on how to handle race discrimination cases. In 2001 a new rule was introduced which enables the union to 'censure and ultimately expel members who are guilty of discriminating behaviour' (UCU 2003: 3).

The union is also involved in researching, writing and publishing many issues on race. It has published a 'toolkit, on campaigning against racism' on its website: *Guidance with Unison on Implementing the Race Relations Amendment Act*. Many articles on race have been published in *The Lecturer* (UCU's newspaper, which is sent to all its members). The union has researched and published a detailed document, *Handling Discrimination Claims and Race and Reputation* (UCU 2003).

In 2005 UCU held its first event for Black History Month. It was organized by the union's Black Staff group. The union had for years supported Black History Month, but in October 2005 they held their own event. 'Grenada' was the subject of discussion along with Bernard Coard's book, *How the West Indian Child is Made Educationally Subnormal in the British Education System*.

UCU is also involved in other positive action. Along with the AUT, the CRE, the Disability Rights Commission and the Equal Opportunities Commission, UCU is in a joint campaign to end pay inequalities in higher education. They will be seeking for equal pay audits and race impact assessment to be carried out in every university and HE college in 2006 (*The Lecturer*, December 2005).

Summary

In this chapter we looked at those who is responsible for promoting and managing race and diversity in FE. We found that there was a great deal of resistance against changing the status quo. All kinds of excuses have been given by managers as to why they cannot change.

Governors who are supposed to police the RRAA 2000 and other equality Acts are sometimes ignorant of their responsibilities. We have argued that both managers and governors need race awareness and diversity training which should point out the responsibility of managers and governors to comply with the equality laws. We have also given practical advice on how colleges can increase the numbers of governors from BME groups.

We have looked at UCU, the staff unions and the changes that they have made in their response to the RRAA 2000 and other equality Acts. We have also looked at HE institutions and how they are promoting the RRAA 2000.

Conclusion

The issues discussed in this book are centred around the Race Relations Amendment Act 2000 and whether FE colleges are implementing it. This led to the examination of institutional racism in the education system since the arrival of black immigrants in Britain in the 1960s. Since then, we have had several Race Acts which have done little to stop the tide of racism in our schools, colleges, universities and in society as a whole.

The RRAA 2000 was designed to eliminate discrimination in our education system and in all public bodies. What is different about this Act is that it gives practical advice on how to meet the general and specific duties outlined in order to promote race equality.

The evidence so far is that, while some FE colleges are taking the RRAA seriously, it is underused by others and has been dropped down their list of priorities. The situation has become so serious in some colleges that the CRE chief, Trevor Phillips, has warned colleges that they must comply with the Act or face compliance orders.

The Commission for Black Staff in FE found overwhelming evidence that many colleges were wittingly or unwittingly discriminating against BME staff and learners. The RRAA 2000 has offered a way out. It asks for colleges to promote race equality by preparing a race equality policy, undertaking monitoring of staff and students by ethnicity, carrying out impact assessment and providing race equality training for all staff. But like all the other Acts designed to eliminate racism, there has been resistance by those who have the power to change the situation. This may be because they are unable, or unwilling, to relate to the suffering caused by racism that is experienced by individuals, groups and countries.

The problem is that people from BME groups who have experience in and understanding of racism do not have the power to change the situation. Those who pass laws do so with the assumption that everyone involved will support equality and diversity and so have not taken into consideration the differing views on the subject.

The RRAA 2000 is resisted by colleges in several ways. While most have the basic requirement – a race policy – many are not promoting it. Some colleges, especially those in predominantly white areas, do not have a race policy. Some colleges monitor staff by ethnicity, but not learners, while others do not act on the result of monitoring, which is the whole point of the operation.

Promoting race equality in order to eliminate discrimination needs commitment by those who have the power to change the situation. While some argue that race initiatives perpetuate rather than diminish the situation, the risk has to be taken. The alternative would be to do nothing, which is indefensible on moral, educational and business grounds.

Bibliography

Abbott, D. (1989) 'Young, gifted and black' in Macguire, S. (ed.) *Transforming Moments*, London: Virago.

Ainley, B. (1994) 'Blacks and Asians in the British media: A study of discrimination', PhD thesis, London: London School of Economics and Political Science.

Ainley, B. (1998) *Black Journalist White Media*, Stoke on Trent: Trentham Books.

Black Leadership Initiative (2004) *Leadership and Diversity – Changing Organisational Cultures*, A Conference Report, London: Black Leadership Initiative.

Black Scientists and Inventors (1998) Black in Science Series, London: BIS Publications.

Black Training and Enterprise Groups Ltd (2005) *Race Equality Work in Further Education Colleges*, Coventry: LSC.

Carby, H. (1982) *Schooling in Babylon, in the Centre for Contemporary Cultural Studies – The Empire Strikes Back*, London: Hutchinson.

Challender, C. (1997) *Education for Empowerment: The Practice and Philosophies of Black Teachers*, Stoke on Trent: Trentham Books.

Coard, B. (1971) *How the West Indian Child is Made Educationally Subnormal in the British Education System*, London: New Beacon Books.

Cohen, L. and Manion, L. (1983) *Multicultural Classroom*, London: Croom Helm.

Colley, H. (2003) *Mentoring for Social Inclusion: A Critical Approach to Nurturing Mentor Relationships*, London: Routledge Falmer.

Commission for Black Staff in Further Education (2002) *Challenging Racism: Further Education Leading the Way*, London: The Commission for Black Staff in Further Education.

Commission for Black Staff in Further Education (2003a) *Race Equality Work in Further Education Colleges: Keeping people who want to stay*, London: The Commission for Black Staff in Further Education.

Commission for Black Staff in Further Education (2003b) *Good*

Practice Guide, Training People Who Want To Know, London: The Commission for Black Staff in Further Education.

CRE (2002) *The Duty to Promote Race Equality: A Guide for Further and Higher Education*, London: CRE.

CRE (2004) *From Issues to Outcomes: Further and Higher Education Institutions: A Guide to Race Equality*, London: CRE.

Dass, P. and Parker, B. (1999) 'Strategies for managing human resource diversity from resistance to learning' in *Academy of Management Executive* 13 (2): 68–80.

DfES (2002) *Success for All: Reforming Further Education and Training*, Nottinghamshire: DfES.

DfES (2003) *DfES Statistical First Release*, Nottinghamshire: DfES.

Education Commission (2005) *The Educational Experiences and Achievements of Black Boys in London Schools 2000–2003*, London: LDA Education Commission.

Foster, A. (2005) *Realising the Potential: A Review of the Future Role of Further Education Colleges*, Nottinghamshire: DfES.

Freedman, M. (1999) *The Kindness of Strangers: Adult Mentors, Urban Youth and the New Voluntarism*, Cambridge: Cambridge University Press.

Fryer, P. (1984) *Staying Power, The History of Black People in Britain*, London: Pluto Press.

Gaine, C. (1998) *No Problem Here, A Practical Approach to Education and Race in White Schools*, London: Hutchinson.

Gilborn, D. (1990) *Race Ethnicity and Education*, London: Unwin Hyman.

Gordon, P. and Rosenberg, D. (1989) *The Press and Black People in Britain*, London: The Runnymede Trust.

Katz, J. (1978) *White Awareness*, Novman, OK: Oklahoma University Press.

Leicester, M. (1993) *Race for a Change in Continuing and Higher Education*, Milton Keynes: SRHE/Open University Press.

Lorbiecki, A. and Jack, G. (2000) 'Critical turns in the evolution of diversity management', *British Journal of Management* 11(3): 17–31.

LSC (2001) *Seeking the Views of Learners, Findings from the LSC's First National Learner Satisfaction Survey*, Coventry: LSC.

LSC (2004) *Evaluation of the Black Leadership Initiative*, Coventry: LSC.

LSRC (2005) *Leadership, Development and Diversity in the Learning and Skills Sector*, Research Report London: LSRC.

Mac an Ghaill, M. (1988) *Young Gifted and Black: Teacher relationships in the schooling of black youth*, Milton Keynes: Open University Press.

Macpherson, P. (1999) *'Racism' in The Stephen Lawrence Inquiry*, London: HMSO.

Mullard, C. (1982) 'Multicultural education in Britain: from assimilation to cultural pluralisms' in Tierney, J. (ed.) *Race Migration and Schooling*, London: Holt, Rinehart and Winston.

Newnham, J. and Watts, S. (1984) *Developing a Multicultural Science Curriculum in Education for a Multicultural Society, Cases Studies in ILEA Schools*, London: Bell & Hoffman.

Olser, A. (1997) *The Education and Careers of Black Teachers: Changing Identities, Changing Lives*, Buckingham: Open University Press.

Rampton, A. (1998) *West Indian Children in Our schools: Interim Report of the Committee of Inquiry into the Education of Children*, Ethnic Minority Groups Series, CMND 8273, London: HMSO.

Rothon, C. and Heath, A. (2003) *Trends in Racial Prejudice in British Social Attitudes*, London: Sage Publications.

Runnymede Trust (2003) *Black and Ethnic Minority Young People and Education Disadvantages*, London: Runnymede Trust.

Scruton, R. (1986) 'The myth of cultural relativism' in Palmers, F. (ed.) *An Assault on Education and Value*, London: Sherwood Press.

Sewell, T. (1997) *Black Masculinities and Schooling. How Black Boys Survive Modern Schooling*, Stoke on Trent: Trentham Books.

Stone, M. (1981) *The Education of the Black Child in Britain: The Myth of Multicultural Education*, London: Fontana.

Swann, M. (1985) *Education for All: Final Report of the Committee of Inquiry into the Education of Children*, Ethnic Minority Groups Series, CMND, 9453, London: HMSO.

Tomlinson, S. (1983) 'Black women in higher education, case studies of university women in Britain' in Barton, L. and Walker, S. (eds) *Race, Class and Education*, London: Croom Helm.

Tomlinson, S. (1984) *Home and School in Multicultural Britain*, London: Batsford.

Troyna, B. (1982) 'The ideological and policy response to black pupils in British schools' in Hartnett, A. (ed.) *The Social Sciences in Educational Studies*, London: Heinemann.

Troyna, B. and Williams, J. (1986) *Racism, Education and the State*, Beckenham: Croom Helm.

UCEA (2004) *Race Equality Toolkit*, London: Universities and Colleges Employer Association.

UCU (1995) *Harassment at Work: How to deal with it?* London: UCU.

UCU (2002) *Discrimination on the Grounds of Religion or Belief*, London: UCU.

UCU (2003) *Response from UCU to the Recommendations of the Commission for Black Staff in Further Education to Trade Unions*, London: UCU.

UCU/Unison (2004) *Implementing the Race Relations Amendment Act, A UCU/Unison Guide*, London: UCU.

Newspaper articles

Bunting, C. (2004) 'Distinct lack of ebony', *The Times Higher Educational Supplement*, 22 October.

Christian, M. (2005) 'Why we go abroad? There are no opportunities for us in Britain', *The Times Higher Educational Supplement*, 4 March.

Clancy, J. (2005) 'Recruit black staff or else: CRE chief Trevor Phillips threatens to force colleges to act on race', *The Times Higher Educational Supplement*, 20 January.

Curtis, P. (2005) 'Jobs for the white boys', Education Guardian, *Guardian*, 22 November.

Davey, A. (2003) 'Underachievement by ethnic minority pupils should not be blamed on teachers only', *Guardian*, 25 March.

Garner, M. (2004) 'The doors to the mainstream are shut to pioneers', *The Times Higher Educational Supplement*, 14 February.

Grace, J. (2004) 'We remain almost invisible', Education: Guardian Higher, *Guardian*, 14 February.

Kingston, P. (2005) 'Opportunity blocks', Education: Guardian Further, *Guardian*, 31 May.

Pope, S. (2005) 'Real life imitates thug life: why gangsta rap is evil as slavery', *New Nation*, 18 April.

Wainwright, T. (2005) 'Luton leads the field in diversity on campus', *The Times Higher Education Supplement*, 15 July.

Resources

Websites

- The Black Presence in Britain
www.blackpresence.co.uk/history
- Caribbean Studies, Black and Asian History (CASBAH)
www.casbah.ac.uk/
- Disability Rights Commission
www.drc-gb.org/drc
- Equal Opportunities Commission
www.eoc.org.uk
- Every Generation
(contains information about black heritage and genealogy)
www.everygeneration.co.uk
- Higher Education Academy
www.heacademy.ac.uk
- Home Office
(links to Human Rights Unit and Race Equality and Diversity Unit)
www.homeoffice.gov.uk
- Kamat's Pot-pourri
(a portal into India's history and complexity)
www.kamat.com
- Learning and Skills Council
www.lsc.gov.uk
- Learning and Skills Development Agency
www.lsda.org.uk
- Network for Black Managers
www.feoline.net
- Niace Racially Inclusive Network
www.niace.org.uk

• The Refugee Council
www.refugeecouncil.org.uk
• UCU
www.ucu.org.uk
• The 1990 Trust
www.blink.org.uk

Education and training resources

African Caribbean Network for Science and Technology
National Head Office
Unit 9 Progress Centre
Cakebread Street
Ardwick Green
Manchester
M12 6HS
www.ishangohouse.com

Black Training and Enterprise Group (BTEG)
Regents Wharf
8 All Saints Street
London N1 9RL
Tel: 0207 713 6161
Fax: 02078370269
www.bteg.co.uk

Development Education Association (DEA)
33 Corsham Street
London
N1 6DR
Tel: 0207 490 8108
www.dea.org.uk

Ethnic Minority Media List
The Media Office, The Commission for Racial Equality
St Dunstan's House
201–211 Borough High Street
London
SE1 1GZ
www.cre.gov.uk

The Runnymede Trust
Suite 106, The London Fruit and Wool Exchange
Brushfield Street
London
E1 63P
Tel: 0207 377 9222
Fax: 0207 377 6622
www.runnymedetrust.org

Index